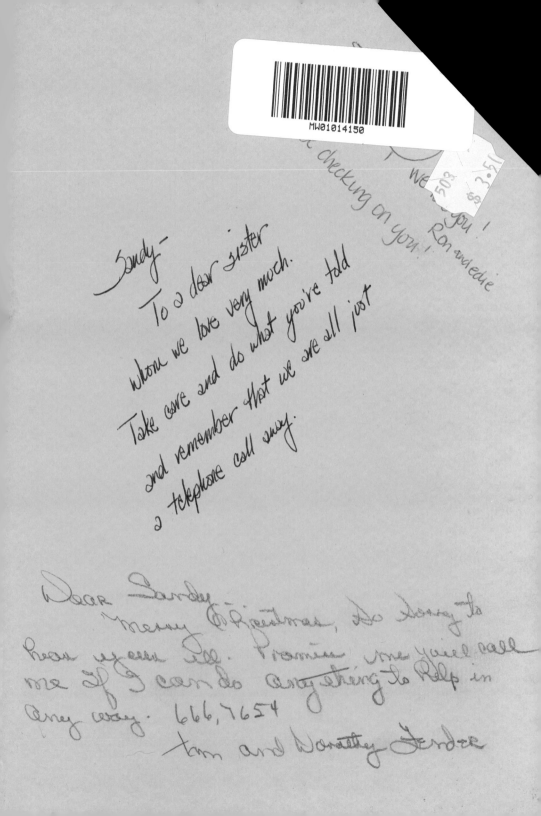

Sandy —
To a dear sister
whom we love very much.
Take care and do what you're told
and remember that we are all just
a telephone call away.

We love you!
Ron and Edie

checking on you!

Dear Sandy —
Merry Christmas. So sorry to
hear you're ill. Promise me you'll call
me if I can do anything to help in
any way. 666-7654
Tom and Dorothy Jordan

LIFE
One to a Customer

LIFE

One to a Customer

Elaine Cannon

BOOKCRAFT · SALT LAKE CITY, UTAH

Library of Congress Catalog Card Number: 81-68131
ISBN O-88494-428-X

5 6 7 8 9 10   89 88 87 86 85 84

Lithographed in the United States of America
PUBLISHERS PRESS
Salt Lake City, Utah

Contents

Growing

Life—One to a Customer

A lot of people have said the same thing in different ways about living fully, living now, and making it a joy forever in the process. For example:

> Today is the first day of the rest of your life.
>
> This is your one chance to live—make it!
>
> Make the most out of what you have to work with.
>
> This is the day the Lord hath made; rejoice and be glad in it!
>
> To every thing there is a season and a time to every purpose under heaven; a time to be born and a time to die; . . . now is your time.
>
> Every day is part of eternity. What happens here and now is forever important.
>
> What is opportunity to the man who can't use it?
>
> Look to this day, for it is the very life of life.

A person can have two serves the first time around in volleyball. Sometimes even the law gives an offender a second chance; but when it comes to living, this is it. Life comes one to a customer.

Scientists have succeeded in assembling all the components of a human being in a test tube. But life doesn't ignite, generate, erupt, explode, self-start, spontaneously combust, or suddenly happen. Life, the essence of life and the timing of the spirit child of God entering its mortal body, is a gift from God. It is under his control. Make no mistake about that.

Have you ever thought why murder and sexual impurity are the two worst sins a person can commit? It is because they deal with life—the beginning of it and the ending of it. Birth and death. To take either life or death into our own hands inappropriately is to play God, usurp his power, take his role. That is a terrible mockery. And it is a grievous sin.

Man has succeeded in effecting some rather impressive substitutes for parts of the body, we'll admit. There is a heart pacer, a kidney machine, an artificial hand that looks about like the real thing, or a metal clawlike prosthesis that can work almost as well as a human hand once you get the hang of it. Artificial legs help people with problems. Wigs, hearing aids, false teeth, and glasses supply amazing replacement for the real thing. Transplants—cornea, kidney, bone, vein, skin, and hair —can work wonders when the need arises.

A seventeen-year-old girl was going blind and suffering acute pain because scar tissue was forming in her eyes. She had been born without tear ducts. The tiny hole in the corner of each eye was missing. Each time she closed her eyes, which we all do so many times a minute, dry surface rubbed against dry surface. And it was excruciatingly painful. Without a tear duct no moisture could be released to lubricate the eyeball. There was no point in removing the scar tissue forming (like a callus on your hand when you rub it against a ball bat the first time in the season), because it would just build up again.

A resourceful specialist finally was able to successfully perform a tricky operation that restored her sight by solving her problem. With the aid of a powerful microscope he shifted a tiny saliva duct (invisible to the naked eye) from the inside of each cheek up along the inside of each side of her nose. Then he sewed each duct into a new hole he'd made in the corner of each eye. At last, tear ducts! Rumor has it that each time she sees a pickle her eyes water, but nonetheless there is now lubrication for her eyes. Her sight is restored through tear ducts almost as fine as if she'd been born with them.

Yes, science has done amazing things to aid God. There are good substitutes or reasonable facsimilies of the real things in human life. But for life itself there is no substitute, no replacement for, no reasonable facsimile of God's gift.

Life—that miraculous happening where a spirit suddenly inhabits a mortal body prepared by the coming together of a male and female—comes to each of us once. And it lasts forever, with one slight variation called death that moves us from this phase to yet another.

No wonder we all want to make such a marvelous success of it!

Once we get going on ourselves, tackling the mote in our own eyes, the world suddenly becomes a little better for everybody else. Oh, what a ripple on the public pond when just one soul gets working on himself!

This is the excitement of life! It is its provocation and its promise.

Since childhood I have recited a little verse with much sense to it:

> I am only one,
> But I am one.
> I can't do everything,
> But I can do something.
> And what I can do
> I ought to do.
> And what I ought to do,
> By the grace of God
> I will do.

Though life is a one-time adventure, we can, by the grace of God, do anything we need to about it, to ensure that it is a successful eternal experience.

Those Who Sin Differently

Longfellow wrote that a single conversation across the table with a wise man is better than ten years' study of books.

Henry Eyring is a wise man as well as a world-famous scientist. He has been honored by kings, cited by scientific societies, published in professional journals, awarded honorary degrees and titles. He is sought after on the lecture circuit. He has knowledge; he has wisdom; he has an infectious sense of humor that reflects his deep sensitivity to life.

He also walks to work and can outlast jogging companions thirty years younger than he. Dr. Eyring is an interesting and fit man.

To have juggled professional demands and human relationships so successfully makes Dr. Eyring a subject worth our looking into. If we attend one of his lectures, we'll learn the scope and meaning of the universe and how an atom explodes. His discoveries have won him prizes, but his caring has brought him friends by the score. Have dinner with Dr. Eyring and you learn what makes him a memorable human being. He will talk about you. Then the next time you meet, there will be a quick rundown of your family tree, your place of roots, your genealogical connections. Dr. Eyring cares about people.

And Dr. Eyring believes in God.

He is a devoted worker in religious circles, helping people find appropriate directions and valid answers to eternal questions, and encouraging faith when answers aren't available yet. To Dr. Eyring, science and religion are not irreconcilable but are, in fact, mutually supporting when one's understanding has gone far enough. This is the basis of Dr. Eyring's personal philosophy of life: The Lord created the universe with eternal laws; personal relationships to be enriching must be based on eternal principles, too.

On one occasion a group of us were talking about a person we all knew who had a particularly difficult personality problem. Suddenly Dr. Eyring changed the tone of the talk with this comment, "I hope I will always be tolerant of those who sin differently from me."

Oh, Dr. Eyring wasn't only talking about those blatant, cardinal wrongdoings we all try to avoid. He was suggesting the importance of keeping the second great commandment and oft-repeated counsel from God to love each other—imperfect though we might be. And that goes for loving our enemies, too.

"Those who sin differently . . ." What a revelation into a man's motivation! What a secret to the implementation of good relationships in our own lives!

Such an attitude emphasizes the truth that none of us is perfection personified—yet. We need to be patient with ourselves as we daily work at overcoming our weaknesses.

The scriptures remind us of that with the words "continue in patience until ye are perfected." (D&C 68:13.) We also will be happier with each other if we develop patience toward others while they struggle with their personal progress, always trying to be tolerant of someone who "sins differently from us."

The inimitable Robert Frost sums it up with these lines from "The Star-Splitter":

If one by one we counted people out
For the least sin, it wouldn't take us long
To get so we had no one left to live with,
For to be social is to be forgiving.

But Dr. Eyring doesn't merely *tolerate* others, remember. He seeks to know them better. With knowledge comes understanding, and the miracle of love comes next.

Elizabeth Mauske had a personal experience that enriched her life and points up for the rest of us that friendship brings out the best in people.

"On her frequent trips on foot to Central America, an old native Indian woman used always to bring my mother a few partridge eggs or a handful of berries. My mother spoke no Araucanian beyond the greeting 'mai-mai,' and the old woman knew no Spanish, but she drank tea and ate cake with many an appreciative giggle. We girls stared fascinated at her layers of colorful hand-woven clothing, her copper bracelets and coin necklaces, and we vied with each other in trying to memorize the singsong phrase she always spoke on rising to leave.

"At last we learned the words by heart and repeated them to the missionary, who translated them for us. They have stayed in my mind as the nicest compliment ever uttered: 'I shall come again, for I like myself when I'm near you.' "

Such acceptance lets us rise above confusion of tongues, differences in cultural backgrounds, and habits bound by tradition. It not only lets us be tolerant of those who sin differently or dress differently or eat differently or vote differently, but it allows us to value others *because* of those very differences.

And it importantly reminds us that while others may not be perfect from our point of view, we aren't perfect yet either.

In Matthew we read: "Judge not, that ye be not judged. For with what judgment ye judge, ye shall be judged: and with what measure ye mete, it shall be measured to you again." (Matthew 7:1-2.)

Real Christian living is more than abstaining from doing things no thoughtful person would think of doing anyway. Real Christian living ought to be doing things that might not occur to anyone who hasn't been touched by Christ.

Henry Eyring bases his behavior on Christ's teachings, and many wonderful people across the land, from Araucanian Indians to hardy Canadians, do the same.

Self-Control

Thomas Jefferson said that nothing gives one person so much advantage over another as to remain always cool and unruffled under all circumstances.

Many have waxed eloquent on this topic. For example, Seneca wrote, "To master oneself is the greatest mastery."

Aristotle said: "I count him braver who overcomes his desires than him who conquers his enemies; for the hardest victory is the victory over self."

And Browning penned: "When the fight begins within himself, a man's worth something."

"The virtue of all achievement is victory over self," wrote A. J. Cronin. And Edgar A. Guest expressed such thoughts in verse:

> I have to live with myself, and so
> I want to be fit for myself to know;
> I want to be able, as days go by,
> Always to look myself straight in the eye.
> I don't want to stand with the setting sun
> And hate myself for the things I've done.

Everyone gives his life for something, whether it is little or much. Joan of Arc was burned at the stake for her beliefs. We aren't all asked to die the martyr's death by being burned alive like Joan of Arc. Nor are we marched into the lion's den these days because of our convictions. But all of us can be sorely tried at a time when we are challenged, embarrassed, judged unfairly, insulted, taunted, ridiculed, or angered. We may find that our principles or needs are quite different from those of our peers. We may need to diet or budget or break some nagging habit. We may need to give up our own interests for the needs of another. Our tempers, patience, or character can be tested smartly even at a change of a circumstance. People are mature or immature depending on how they react to what life thrusts upon them; but because we cannot always direct events, we must learn self-control—to govern ourselves. If we fail in responding appropriately to life's challenges, we pay a high price.

The Bible tells us that "as [a man] thinketh in his heart, so is he." (Proverbs 27:3.) Another maxim is that acting as though you are, can make you that way. And another is that thinking begets behavior which begets character. All of these remind us that we ought to do some thinking about what we can take and what we can give and what we can give up. The journey of all the rest of our lives is affected by how we handle ourselves today.

The concept of self-control (or the lack of it) surfaced generations ago. It all began when Eve hearkened to the voice of the tempter and ate the forbidden fruit. She then confessed before God's questionings, "The serpent beguiled me, and I did eat." (Genesis 3:13.) Often since then we have been busily blaming someone else or some circumstance for our own weaknesses.

It is true that environment and even heredity have some force in a person's actions and decisions. But always there is the element of choice. Here is a truth that we can lean to —we can be master of our fate. We *can* lose weight, quit swearing, save money, get organized. We can do anything we want to if we want to badly enough.

We can learn to control our attitude about things we can't do anything else about, too.

I stood on the corner with a teenage boy who was blind. He paused a moment and then stepped into the traffic. I cautioned him to wait until the light changed. Hearing me speak, he turned my way and smiled broadly: "Oh, thank you. With this wind blowing, it's hard to hear the cars coming. We've been trained to listen to the traffic pattern since we can't see the semaphores."

And knowing I was there, he began a friendly visit which lasted until we reached the blind center a block away. He told me he had lost his sight at age eight when he had been struck across his eyes with a ball bat. There had been months into years of tears and despair while a little boy learned to adjust to a terrible personal tragedy.

"How have you finally come to such a positive outlook?" I asked.

"One day my father was helping me fly my kite, and it became caught in the tree. When he finally got it for me, I was terribly upset because it was broken; and I cried out to my father over and over again, 'Fix it!' 'Fix it!' But he could not. He moved my hands across the torn paper and the splintered wood, the tangled string. 'It cannot be fixed, son,' my father said. 'Like your eyes, it cannot be fixed.' And suddenly I knew it was hopeless. I really couldn't fly my kite anymore. We'd have to do something else. And in that same moment I knew I'd never see again. I'd have to get along without sight. I guess I grew up then. Well, here I am—I can tell by the stones especially pebbling the walk in front of the center. Thanks, and make it a good day!"

Such wisdom from one so young and so handicapped is wisdom we can surely take to heart. There are some things we can do something about, like making it a good day no matter what, and some things we just have to accept and adjust to. And we ought to be making a good day of it with the time we have.

Each of us has his problems, his cross to bear, a lemon that has been handed him unbidden. Most of us have created some intricacies in our lives by foolish behavior, careless decisions, or thoughtless conversation. We can repent and try harder to understand, to reason through why we reacted as we did. It helps if we look to the lives of others and how they reacted.

Joan of Arc was burned, and tradition has it that she didn't flinch. In 1844 Joseph Smith was shot by a mob in Carthage, Illinois, for his efforts to restore the full teachings of God within a new church. He went, as he said, "like a lamb to the slaughter." Jesus Christ was crucified, and he prayed to God, "Forgive them; for they know not what they do." (Luke 23:34.)

These are supreme examples of noble control. As Seneca said, "To master oneself is the greatest mastery."

I believe this with all my heart. Don't you, really?

Change

Homecoming events, class reunions, and treks to the scenes of our childhood are nostalgic affairs at best, but they prove one thing: Life is full of change. Thomas Wolfe put it into words for us when he said, "You can't go home again." That's true in the sense that he meant it, of course, but just because things won't be the way they were, should the pilgrimage be abandoned? Or could a new perspective of old ways actually be enriching?

It's something to think about.

Change is the one certainty in life and one of the hardest things for us to cope with.

When I had my first baby about thirty years ago, my life-style changed. I was treated with great respect and infinite tenderness. My husband was appropriately anxious. The medical staff of the hospital hovered over me by the minute. My mother, who had conducted the affairs of my own arrival in her bed at home, stood by with the kind of maternal anxiety I had consciously witnessed in her on only one other occasion. That was when I was to perform at my first piano recital before some of her friends. Now I was to rise to the occasion and put on a proper performance again.

I stayed in that hospital bed for ten days, scarcely lifting my arm other than to hold the baby at feeding time. Then I moved home to mother's for further pampering. I wasn't an invalid. I was just treated like one. That's how it was done then.

But things change. Twelve or so years after the

first baby, our last child was born. By then, having a baby was a rather simple arrangement. I was home from the hospital cooking waffles again for our little destroying angels almost before I could cry out for joy.

Yes, change is inevitable. There is social change, physical change, environmental change, ideology change. We are skinny and then saggy. We are young, and we get old. We learn our way around town, and the freeway comes. We are single and then married. We are born, we die. We laugh, we cry. We are relaxed, and a new responsibility comes. Crickets sing in the summer night, and suddenly it is Christmas.

Sometimes change comes swiftly, startlingly. Sometimes its pace is so gradual as to be almost imperceptible. It is subtle and secret, unnoticed until it is too late. Sometimes change is announced, painful, dramatic. Sometimes change is the best thing ever to happen, bringing its own blessings. But sometimes it really hurts. Giving up the comfortably familiar and facing the unknown can create stress.

Well, ready or not, fate seems to cry, you shall be caught—by change.

Some people handle change well, some with less success and a considerable short-circuiting of their power. If we look around us we'll see many examples. A family moves to a new school district, and a child withdraws in the face of the threat of all those new faces in class. A man loses his wife, and a once perfectly charming person becomes a bore worshipping at the altar of the deceased.

Change is pain, but change is learning. So how can we effectively cope with it? What attitude will we assume when we are facing a negative trauma instead of a joyful moment in change? Isn't it a matter of the proverbial lemon and the ade, after all? We may not be able to change circumstances, but we can control our responses to them. We make lemonade out of the lemon life hands us.

It helps to direct one's thinking by asking questions such as: "How can I take this with grace?" or "What lesson can I learn from this?" or "Which of my Heavenly Father's principles will help me now?"

The answers to these questions come in knowing that those eternal principles are laws irrevocably decreed in heaven before this earth existed, upon which all blessings are predicated. If we want the blessing, we must live the law governing it. (See D&C 130:20-21.) A change may benefit us greatly when we learn the truth about it and act upon the governing law. We take the law irrevocably decreed and match it against the challenge of a particular change. It works. Live the law, reap the blessing.

My own secret feeling about life is that it is a wonderful adventure to experience deeply. When change comes, welcome it as a new adventure. Or face it with curiosity, at least. Get involved. Record details in a journal. Live it all the way. For example, make friends with the seasons rather than storming about storms. Dress for it and go forth to experience snow in your face. Breathe the spring and press petals of summer; caress a baby's softness, but stroke the wrinkles of age while marveling at the plan of life. It is enriching.

This is how I feel, at any rate. Let me experience change so I can understand more, is my cry. Let me cope so I can qualify for eternal life.

I've lived a while now. Having babies isn't part of my life's business anymore. Loving them still is, of course, and so is helping them to understand what I am just beginning to value so highly. When you deal with it according to God's eternal principles, change is joy.

With Your Hand in God's

Sloshing through sticky leaves in a rainstorm, arms locked and heads bowed, we talked about "cabbages and kings," my friend and I. Small talk with deep implications. The setting was perfect for it. We were unselfconscious in our expressions because our prime purpose was to keep from slipping on the sog. The rain triggered our talk to Noah and his ark—Noah, who, while men scoffed, obeyed God and won. Then we moved to King David, who didn't. Sobering to think about, isn't it?

There are powerful lessons for all of us to learn from the lives of our biblical friends. Consider the story of David, the Shepherd Boy, who became David, the King.

The scriptures report that David, the Shepherd Boy, was anointed in the midst of his brethren, and the Spirit of the Lord came upon David from that day forward. They go on to say that David behaved himself wisely in all his ways, and the Lord was with him, and his name was much set by from the fields to the places of honor.

David, the Shepherd Boy, put his hand in God's, and a marvelous kind of miracle happened. While seasoned warriors quailed and watched, David slew a giant with a stone.

But David, the King, took his hand from God's and committed a crime. While no one watched, he slew a warrior and took that warrior's wife. In secret he was responsible for a warrior's death. And that made all the difference for the rest of his life.

Like David, we each have a path to walk, a mission to fill, and promises to keep. We can seek the solitude of the shepherd, revel in a closeness to earth and the creatures of earth so that we feel near God and let his Spirit come upon us. We can consider the giants in our lives as well as the places of honor to strive for. With our hand in God's we can work our dreams into reality.

But this requires a certain kind of battle with self, doesn't it, to keep our hand in God's when there are so many distractions and pulls?

You know about battles. There are all kinds of them. Team tactics you have an inkling of. Athletic events with their scoreboards are familiar. Civil war you've learned about in school. Tug-of-war is a game from childhood that has a carry-over into adult life and decision-making.

You can go along, for a time, as a sweet innocent, fresh from baptism and radiant as the dawn. You can cling to your parents with proper obedience, for a time. You can memorize the words of God and recite them at family gatherings or shine in seminary or Sunday school. You can fold your arms in prayer at church and feel virtuous inside. You might even marvel at the might of one like David when it is story-telling time. All is well, for a time.

Then one day, life is upon you. You are out in the big world thinking for yourself. The time for decision, for action, now can't be thrust back upon the prophet or the parent or anybody else. Dad isn't beside you in the car. Mom isn't part of the scene when the crowd gets wickedly lively. God won't interfere when you are being sorely tempted. Life is testing, you know. Sabbath-day sermons are forgotten. The word of God seems to have little to do with passing exams or falling in love or running a business. And when peer pressure or stark ideologies surface excitingly, it's reality, upper case.

After all, David's first problem was only a giant. Your foe might be your best friend whose ideals aren't as high as yours. Soon we learn that good intentions aren't going to help win the battle with self. The dilemma is shifting from depending upon the arm and mind of others to self-accountability with one's hand in God's. This is what the battle is all about.

Psychologists and religionists have suggested our getting a mental picture of our best self. Dr. Maxwell Maltz in his book *Psychocybernetics* prescribes a thirty-minute mental exercise of seeing self as the way we want to be, moving and choosing and performing according to our best self-image. Tennyson observed long ago that "self-reverence, self-knowledge, self-control, these three alone lead life to sovereign power."

It also helps to remember that God created man and set up the system we're currently living under. He has pinpointed the principles to get us through. They are tried and true —the formulas, the recipes, the theorems, the rules of the game, the laws for quality life and personal joy. Nothing else works. Man-made signals can't touch those of the Creator of man.

The culminating and most motivating guide in the battle for self-control is "Thy will not mine, O Lord." This is the commitment we make when we put our hand into his and we feel that comfort of being cared for by one who is all wise and good, who loves us and knows us better than we do ourselves. His will is the best for us in the long run. He created us.

Now, to abide by God's will we have to know it, don't we? This suggests a prayerful study of his word plus determined application of it to life.

Then, like David, the Shepherd Boy, we can reach for all the blessings available to us through the laying on of hands by God's servants. Under these circumstances being a winner is a distinct probability.

David, though he became king, lost all that he had won when he ceased to live by God's will. His problems began not when he faced the giant, but when he took his hand from God's.

And so it is with us.

Women as an Influence

There are two important days in a woman's life: the day she is born and the day she finds out why. She has just one chance to live on earth—like everybody else. To secure the satisfying life as a bachelor-girl, as a bride, as a grandmother —even as a beginning young woman—she must put into play her every strength, wisdom, wile, talent, and prayer.

We've all heard about the beauty and charm of a bride. There she goes, the misty-eyed bride enveloped in veils of romance, hope, dreams, modesty, allure, and nest building. Her cup runneth over with love. With her hand in the Lord's and her heart in her husband, she moves forward to the adventure of life. And, ideally, one day she will have her hand in her husband's and her heart in the Lord.

This change, of course, is what life is all about.

How does it all happen? What factors make a woman's life what she wants it to be?

A woman whose attitude is mellowed by a closeness to God, whose life is sweetened by gospel experiences, a woman enlightened by religious training, strengthened by saving ordinances, and directed by inspired leadership, is bound to have a unique view of why she was born. No matter how broadminded or emancipated, liberated or sophisticated she may claim to be, deep down she knows she is a cherished child of God. She is the recipient, with others of his children both male and female, of all the blessings of a plan of eternal life. The day a woman of any age comes to understand this, to at last be comfortable in God's will for her, is the day she finds out why she was born. It is the day of her own giant step.

The lessons a particular woman has to learn may be different in detail from her sister's. But living to one day claim the fullest of God's promised blessings is every woman's business —or it ought to be.

To learn and grow as a human being is important. To become skilled in one's particular role is the avenue to true fulfillment. Perhaps one of the very good things to come out of the restless Women's Rights movement over the years has been the intellectual awakening that has come to women themselves. This awakening has been an excuse to consider what it means to be human as well as to be female. For a woman to consider blessings and responsibilities, realities and unchangeables, frameworks and possibilities, is to open a door to fuller living.

Today some women have chosen to enter or been forced into the marketplace, into the mainstream, into the so-called vicissitudes of the hard outside world. Yet if there is to be that precious continuity, the saving sanity, the humanness so necessary to quality life for us all, someone still has to deal with the going to bed, the getting up, the comforting and caring for those with whom we live. It is what women seem especially suited for. It is the reality that the veiled bride must deal with.

It seems unquestionably to be her special stewardship. I personally believe it is her privilege. No matter where her talents, her opportunities, or her situation take her, no matter what her age, really, a woman who cultivates caring about others and influencing them for good is expending her precious energies in a proper way.

In an historical address delivered over one hundred years ago in New York, Elizabeth Cady Stanton had this to say: "If in marriage either party claims the right to stand supreme, to woman, the mother of the race, belongs the scepter and the crown. Her life is one long sacrifice for man. You tell us that among womankind there is no Moses, Christ or Paul—no

Michelangelo, Beethoven, Shakespeare—no Columbus or
Galileo—no Locke or Bacon. Behold those mighty minds so
grand, so comprehensive—they themselves are *our* great works!
In you center our very life, our hopes, our intensest love. For you
we gladly pour out our heart's blood and die, knowing that from
our suffering comes forth a new and more glorious resurrection
of thought and life."

Well, that is some influence, isn't it? And the
bride, trailing her veils behind her, may well be stirred by such
perspective.

Great gifts in women often haven't taken the
form that brings personal recognition or wealth. Somebody is
always needing his hand held, his dinner prepared, her heart
comforted, her nose wiped. Some loved one is forever needing a
good influence to nudge him through multi-pressured society.
And there are only so many hours a day, so much personal
energy, and a few citations—Oscars, Tonys, Emmys, or Nobel
prizes—given to the girl whose life is marked by selflessness.
Maybe that's why the world was so taken when Sister Theresa,
so old and worn and yet so unwearying, was presented the
coveted Nobel recognition. But awards or not, what rare satis-
faction, confirmed by the swelling of the spirit, a person feels
when serving God's children in whatever positive way!

For a bride, a younger girl, a woman of maturity,
or anyone for that matter, to be a humanitarian and a partner
with God in lifting mankind is a noble effort. But to know the
fine details of how to implement this ideal in our own lives is
something else.

What is the key? It seems to be a matter of
quality and goodness, of aliveness and fidelity. The June bride
and her sisters in any season should look to being what women
are especially suited to be, and that is doing great good. To love
a child she has never known, to reach beyond the corners of her
own selfish interest, to play the supporting role to man, to keep

heart in a home, even if she is out of it in the working world—
these make a woman of any age womanly.

It is an exciting effort, too, to develop self so we
can contribute to others, at last having our heart and our hand
in God's.

A View From Above

Getting a view from above of what's going on below has always been fascinating for mankind. Children get excited as they dare each other to climb higher and higher in the apple tree, and little ones squeal in delight at their parents on the ground as their swing takes them up, up, and out of their parents' reach.

People peer from observation decks of skyscrapers and stop their cars at lookout spots at Grand Canyon or Big Sur. Astronauts gaze back upon Earth in awe. But even before the astronauts, carrier pigeons were sent soaring with tiny cameras strapped to their breasts so that man could get a view from above the world on which he lived. The city boy from his stretching fire escape, the native boy with his towering palm tree, the sailor atop the ship's mast, get up and beyond themselves with such vantage points.

One of the favorite tourist spots near Amsterdam is the flower auction, where visitors walk blocks on narrow balconies that circle literally acres of living color in the flower stalls below. Athens from the Parthenon is a white sea as far as the eye can see. How changed the city is when one comes down to mingle in the press of people and their trappings of life!

Scanning the landscape from the window of an in-flight mainliner is fascinating. Exquisite patterns emerge from the tapestry of a Wisconsin farmer's alfalfa field zig-zagged by a narrow avenue of corn stalks. One wonders if he designed it deliberately for the passengers instead of out of some mysterious agricultural need. Pineapple fields in Hawaii laced with roads of coral sands offer a bit of beauty vastly different from Utah's dead sea, the Great Salt Lake, with its surrounding purple and grey mineral markings that frame the red patches of brine shrimp being commercially cultivated for fertilizer. Irrigation pipe tracks in Texas and Idaho have their own distinctive geometric look. The property lines of acreage in England are edged with hedges of stones varying picturesquely from the Orient's rice paddies separated by narrow canals. A California orchard of orange blossoms is a white swath compared to the Sahara's swirling sand dunes.

There is an ancient Chinese proverb that says, "If you don't scale the mountain, you can't see the plain." This is true of our lives. The view from above gives a different perspective, and if we could see ourselves as God sees us, we might work at making our lives different, even better.

I can personally recommend such activity.

I grew up in the Rockies, and our family home was on the foothill of a solitary, beehive-shaped mountain that was a moving force all of my young life. I could see it from my bedroom window and felt a certain security in its closeness. As our family sat at the kitchen table we watched winter skiers mark herringbone trails in fresh snow, and after the first thaw we'd note the progress of spring hikers. I had climbed its bald dome with my family, with church groups, and with a gang of kids (our sack lunches squashed down into the sweaters tied about our waists). Then one day, driven by desire to go to the mount like Moses and commune with God about me—to consider who I was and what I was going to do about it—I set out alone to climb that peak. I was sixteen, and this day my aloneness on the mountain was exhilarating. It was a most spectacular spring morning at sunrise when I made my way to the top. This was no small hill, so the perspective of my neighborhood below reminded me of the soap city I had carved of Salt Lake City when I was twelve.

With fascination I sat looking down at the houses I knew so well and at their people beginning to stir with the sun. Cars backed out, sprinklers splashed on, the trolley clanged up from town. I watched the achingly familiar scenes as an extension of myself. Yet, it was like being God, seeing the whole picture like that. Seeing but not being seen. I followed the paths of my life, from home to friend's house, to the church on the corner and the school down the hill, to the neighborhood store, to a teacher who had touched me. Finally I let myself look upon our own white stucco house, the scene of my most tender times, my most important learnings. Almost in panic I realized how small it looked, and with a wrench of my heart I felt childhood slipping from my grasp.

Everywhere I looked there was someone who had touched my life. At sixteen I was the sum of all of them—parents, school chums, storekeeper, church leader. My heart flooded with a new awareness. Suddenly I realized I had some debts to pay. In 1847 Brigham Young had led a band of pioneers up to the top of that mountain and raised an ensign to the Lord, according to the plaque mounted there. Well, I raised my own standard that day and came down from the mount determined to be useful. The world seemed beautiful, and I was glad to be alive.

Remember Edna St. Vincent Millay's "Oh world, I cannot hold thee close enough"?

God created the world and the world is an exquisite place. Getting a view from the top offers a valuable perspective of how mankind, God's ultimate creation, fits into the scheme of things.

For the song "Awakening" I wrote these words:

Who am I?
What special purpose is mine?
I follow winged sparrows
And I yearn

I yearn to soar
I hear the ocean's thunder
    There is power
    But what am I?
I see lilies blooming
Where the winter storms have swept the field
    I feel the sun
    By its radiance
I see all that God created
I, too, am God's creation
And He knows me as His own
Tenderly I know Him in my heart
Who am I?
I am a child of God.

    And that lofty perspective makes all the difference.

The Gift of Trouble

There is a framed saying in my office that reads: "There is no such thing as a problem without a gift in its hands."

I keep that quote there to remind myself and the people I counsel with that good can come from trouble; blessings are an outgrowth of trials well met; trauma enlivens the heart; clouds have silver linings, and the leaf will burst again on the dry branch.

I once interviewed a remarkable old gentleman who had been confined in a wheelchair since his youth. This was before the time of ramps and parking privileges for the handicapped, or even driving and household equipment that aided the paraplegic. Society largely looked upon anyone who was stricken as different, as an oddity to be avoided—the old gentleman knew all about that. In addition he had lost his wife and family, and he struggled to keep himself going. His livelihood wasn't courtesy of United States government welfare handouts, either.

It was rougher then than it is today.

"You have had trouble all of your life," I said to him. "How have you faced it?"

"Young woman, I don't know what to reply to such a question. I have had nothing but blessings all the days of my life." He smiled warmly.

"But you are in a wheelchair," I insisted. "It is obvious that you have had bad luck. Yet you regard this as a blessing?"

"Why, yes," was his quick and firm reply. "I've been lifted around by some of the best people in the world, and they'd never have paid me a bit of attention otherwise."

He was thoughtful a moment and then he said, "I do remember, however, the day I decided that since I'd never lift anybody in and out of a wheelchair, I would have to do my lifting in my visits with them."

Then came the memorable line, "I have learned that what God said to Abram of old was true for me, too. 'Fear not, Abram: I am thy shield, and thy exceeding great reward.'" (Genesis 15:1.)

Surely that's true of us, too.

Robert Louis Stevenson has long been a favorite author of mine. My mother read me pleasantly to sleep with *The Child's Garden of Verses* and then introduced me to *Treasure Island*. I have recently come to understand what the man really went through to produce his fascinating tales for posterity to enjoy. He recorded in his journal the following: "For fourteen years I have not had a day of real health. I have wakened sick and gone to bed weary, yet I have done my work unflinchingly. I have written in bed and out of bed, written in hemorrhages, written in sickness, written torn by coughing, written when my head swam for weakness—and I have done it all for so long that it seems to me I have won my wager and recovered my glove. Yet the battle still goes on: Ill or well is a trifle so long as it goes. I was made for contest, and the Powers-That-Be have willed that my battlefield shall be the dingy, inglorious one of the bed and the medicine bottle."

Now, we might think that expression to be indicative of compulsion, endurance, courage, or skill in overcoming obstacles. It is all of that, of course. But I'm suggesting it is a paragraph about the good that can come through personal trial —if we'll let it.

I'm going to share with you Ted M. Jacobsen's sensitive reflection on dealing with trauma and terrible testing. It was inspired by his sister Christine's valiant but losing battle with cancer:

"To most every life come solemn, unannounced challenges. Grave, unkind, life-critical challenges. Challenges to the depth and quality of our faith. Tearing at our heart and at the fabric of faith we've woven. We face them haltingly. Then we probe them—first testing their reality and then their resolve. We would not bid them come, or stay; for these test and plumb the very depths of our spirit. They cause at times love to contend with faith—oft times as we struggle thus to find again peace and reason, we may glimpse Gethsemane, then eternity. But as the ripples clear we sense that uninvited challenges have high, refining, eternal purpose. And 'simple' faith is not simple—but is a reflection of both heart and mind, the crown of a righteous trusting life."

I saw the stage play, then the movie, and since have lost myself in a book about the famous "elephant" man who lived near the turn of the century in England. He was a character with a soul so sensitive that his being a freak of nature for men to laugh at was more poignant than it might have been for someone less finely tuned. When he was taken from his sordid carnival environment by compassionate friends and permitted to see some of the beauties in the world, his whole being changed. He seemed more noble and more knowing than ordinary men about him. One day he looked upon only the highest spires of the cathedral beyond the window of his confinement place, and because of the awakening of his soul he was able to build the foundation of the structure purely from his imagination. It became the pattern for his being. He saw the highest spires of his own life at last, and built a new base for his being— far loftier than the original image he had of himself as a freak of nature.

It helps if we look upon life as a preparation for the blessings of eternal life. In this way we can set our sights on different goals. Rather than looking for the happiness badge at the end of each day, we'll be more apt to look for lessons learned. Instead of complaining bitterly, or simply enduring with grace, we can also grow. Instead of noisily shouting, "Why me?" or, "Why now?" we can declare that we are not going to blow this one chance to live by being self-pitying or sulking. We can get on with searching for the truths, the principles to help us deal with the problem appropriately so that one day this trial, too, can be counted as a blessing in disguise.

It is helpful to remember, as Paul pointed out to the Hebrews, that Christ is not unfeeling about our infirmities. He was in all points tried and tested as we now are. Yet he was without sin. He has been through it. He cares. He wants us ultimately to be like him, to make it through the trials, as he did. And he is waiting to be gracious to us.

There is a mighty promise in this scripture: "Lift up your heads and be of comfort . . . I will ease the burdens which are put upon your shoulders, that even you cannot feel them upon your backs, even while you are in bondage; and this I will do that ye may stand as witnesses for me hereafter, and that ye may know of a surety that I, the Lord God, do visit my people in their afflictions." (Mosiah 24:13-14.)

God is able to keep his promises. He does keep them, I know. But since life is a school to learn what the Savior learned, he will not deny us our right to learn for ourselves. He blesses us not in spite of our nagging tests in life, but because of them. He loves us not because we are so great and good yet, but because he is. He is our creator. He prescribed the principles to experience life with. He loves us and wants to help us without taking away our agency.

This is the gift.

An Exercise in Loving

February is a month marked for remembrance of love and friendship. The celebration of hearts and flowers is calendared and crowed about commercially, lest we forget. It is an excuse for an exercise in loving.

And we happily accept this manipulation of our lives as part of the necessary system of organizing and refining the teeming masses—assigned dates to celebrate motherhood, to give thanks for the harvest, to honor the Savior, and to remember our loved ones.

February isn't, of course, the only time we'll dwell on love. It is simply a convenient time to unselfconsciously talk about the subject a bit and maybe learn something to soften stressful times the rest of the year.

Remembering love is like coming in with the tide or suddenly driving into an orchard in full bloom. Paul Engle wrote about the tender trauma of coming upon a loved one unexpectedly. He described that kind of meeting as being almost more than a mere mortal in love could stand. It is as if on a summer day, in the dazzle of noon heat, one snowflake fell on an astonished hand.

To remember love after a season of storm, of bartering in the marketplace, or of dealing with a deteriorating physical body—oh, to remember love in the midst of marriage surrounded by children and personality conflicts or after bouts with selfish sin is to feel wholesome again.

One learns through Shakespeare's words:

Love's not Time's fool . . .
Love alters not with his brief hours and weeks,
But bears it out even to the edge of doom.

So love lasts—it just needs to be remembered, to be uncovered again. We all want to be capable of steady friend-ship and enduring love, and thinking about it can build the warm goodness of heart and strength of mind necessary.

Ashley Montagu, a famous anthropologist, says that love is more than a subjective feeling. It is a series of acts by means of which one person lets another realize that he or she is deeply involved, profoundly interested in their relationship and in that other person's welfare.

For example, a road worker sat eating in the shade of his bulldozer, and he chuckled as he opened one small package in his lunch box. "You do that every day," frowned a co-worker. "You open your lunch and smile."

Sheepishly his friend showed him a hard-cooked egg labeled, "You're a good egg, pop," and then two chocolate kisses taped together on a big red exclamation point.

"My kids and my wife make a big fuss over me. They claim they don't want daddy coming home with his tail between his legs," he explained.

The co-worker was quiet a moment and then confessed, "My wife won't even get out of bed to make me break-fast, let alone a lunch." He threw his own concoction of dry bread and cheese off into the weeds. What truth there is in the oft-quoted statement, 'Love begets love'!

A woman, long-widowed, was planning the happy details of a second marriage. Love had come again. Hesi-tantly she asked her eldest son, college-age now, if he'd give her away at the wedding ceremony. His answer spelled the sweetness of their years. "Give you away? I'm not finished with you yet, mom!"

The kindnesses of love described in Edwin Mark-

ham's old and gentle poem make perfect wording for a valentine
to a special friend or loved one.

> I dare not ask your very all:
> I only ask a part.
> Bring me—when dancers leave the hall—
> Your aching heart.
> Give other friends your lighted face
> The laughter of the years:
> I come to crave a greater grace—
> Bring me your tears!

A companion piece provides still another dimen-
sion to love. It's a little verse I learned so long ago I've forgotten
its source, but it seems to me that today's generation just might
benefit from such a perspective.

> There is a giving beyond giving
> Yours to me
> Who awoke last night
> Hours before the dawn
> Set free
> By one intolerable lightning stroke
> That ripped the sky—
> To understand what love withholds in love
> And why.

Love is a miracle worker. Whether it comes
unbidden or is carefully cultivated, it is the healer, the heaven-
sent blessing as well as the lilt in life. It overcomes deprivations;
it spans the gaps of cultural differences. It rises above barriers of
age; it fills in the blanks between two imperfect people. Love
is the mighty mellower that makes all the difference.

Valentine's Day is a reminder to remember love.
But before Valentine's there was 1 Corinthians chapter 13, and
before Corinthians there was Christ, the blessed model for loving
others. I'll remind you of only brief passages in Paul's classic

statement on love. It seems to be the guidance to follow if we would love as Christ loved and ultimately become as he is.

"Charity suffereth long, and is kind; charity envieth not; charity vaunteth not itself, is not puffed up, doth not behave itself unseemly, seeketh not her own, is not easily provoked, thinketh no evil; rejoiceth not in iniquity, but rejoiceth in the truth." (1 Corinthians 13:4-6.)

How nice that February gives us an excuse for an exercise in loving!

Choosing

So Many Views

You've heard the delightful story about the older man who was concerned about his wife and couldn't get her to see an ear specialist, so he went to the doctor himself and asked for advice on how to handle this problem. The doctor told him to use a simple test. The man was to go home and call to his wife from several places, and if she didn't respond quickly there would be clear evidence of her need for medical help.

The concerned husband went home and called to his wife from the front door, "Ida!" No answer. Then he moved inside and called, "Ida!" Silence. Then he called from the dining room. Still no answer. At last he confronted her in the kitchen. "Ida," he said, "I have been calling you."

And she replied, "I know, my dear, and I have answered you three times."

The problem wasn't Ida's. Isn't this often the case with us?

In First Corinthians we read: "There are . . . so many . . . voices in the world." (1 Corinthians 14:10.) And so we've learned. Whose shall we hear? Hearing can often be our problem not another's, as our gentleman friend learned.

It is, after all, so easy to live in the world after the manner of the world, and it is simple to live alone by your own ideals. The challenge comes in living in the world but not being of it. Sorting out what we listen to, what we hear, and what at last we do is a good move for anyone struggling with peer pressure and worldly influences.

There is a familiar old hymn that echoes these words, "I'll be what you want me to be, dear Lord." When we sing it, we may mean it as we sit in church surrounded by the warm flood of the gospel and the support of fine people. But it isn't always the same afterwards.

When church is over and the sermon is done, voices from the world sometimes confuse us—voices that are coaxing and compelling, louder and jazzier than those at church.

One day I was working at my kitchen sink. The window above it was wide open to let in the springtime. And I could keep an eye and ear on our preschooler son playing in the garden below. Suddenly he and the little girl he was with changed their plans of play. Mischief was surfacing. So I called to him to come in. He didn't come. I called again. No response. I called a third time before I put down my dish towel and went outside to get him.

"Why didn't you answer me?" I confronted him sternly. "Didn't you hear me?"

"Sort of."

"Sort of? Why didn't you come when I called?" I insisted.

And then came the punch line, "But mom, she talked louder. Her mouth was in my ear!"

A teaching moment was at hand. I had to help him understand about voices—about loud voices and small voices, good voices and not-so-good ones, and about whose to listen to when. And why.

Whose voice is it you are hearing? Is it a voice of experience? a voice of excitement? Is it a loving leader's voice? a prayerful parent's plea? Or is it the voice of mischief?—a voice of one who just doesn't understand God's plan?

In trying to determine what voice to listen to, it helps to consider what the voice is telling you to do; what is at stake; what you lose or what you gain; what price you pay in peace, reputation; and what comes next.

Just because a voice is loud, even right in your ear, is no reason to sell your birthright for a mess of pottage or to lose cherished standing because the Lord is temporarily tuned out. It is no reason to make the kind of mistake that delays personal progress.

You see, our little boy ignored my voice and justified it on the basis of "her voice was louder—it was in my ear."

That's surely true. But that voice was leading him astray. He was still a child and hadn't learned the voice-sorting process yet. He hadn't learned to evaluate. Fortunately, he wasn't accountable yet, either. But we all are. We are no longer children who see through the glass darkly. We know better, and the expectations for our performance are higher in the sight of God as well as man.

The effort, then, to cultivate that still small voice is exquisitely important so that we learn to listen to the Lord's will for us. He will not force us into happiness or heaven. Force was the adversary's plan. And that makes all the difference.

There is something I have learned about the Lord's system that can, perhaps, be valuable to you. Sin isn't hurtful because it is forbidden. It is forbidden because it is hurtful. God has not commanded us to abstain from anything except those things that are harmful for us. On the other hand, he knows what will bring us the most joy. Instant gratification isn't on that list. I plead with you to listen to the still small voice that says, "Wait. Not now. Resist. Anticipate. Prepare."

These lines from John Keats's "Ode on a Grecian Urn" relate to this:

> Heard melodies are sweet, but those unheard
> Are sweeter; therefore, ye soft pipes, play on;
> Not to the sensual ear, but, more endeared,
> Pipe to the spirit ditties of no tone.

We have been talking about the many voices

around us. We, too, are part of the voices others hear. What are we saying?

Are we a voice of truth, a voice of gladness, a voice of helpfulness, a voice of righteousness, a voice of love? I pray that we may be, and that we'll be very selective in the voices we listen to.

I want you to listen to my voice now as I testify of the Lord Jesus Christ. He lives. He loves us. He will help us in living our lives and in doing his work—but we must listen to his word or we'll be cunningly and carefully led astray.

It is recorded in John: "He goeth before [us], and [his] sheep . . . know his voice." (John 10:4.)

Out of the many voices around us, may we hear his and may our voices be an echo of his in all the important ways.

Begin the World Again

Thomas Paine wrote, "We have it in our power to begin the world over again." And for me, that is true each January—a chance to begin my world over again and keep an accounting of it in a personal journal.

The beginning of a new year is the time to start a new journal, even if the old one isn't quite finished. It is in keeping with the tradition of turning over a new leaf, of flipping the calendar back to the beginning.

In a new journal all the pages are clean, and the promise of better entries, better living, of surprise experiences lures one to the fresh start.

What will the new year hold? What challenges and simple delights? What separations and comings together? What lessons learned and mistakes made? What insights? What happenings to speak about? What witnesses of God's goodness of which to testify?

Ah, the gift of a new year is a blessed one. A clean, unmarked, unlettered journal rests on the desk before us like a new life.

There is another reason to write a record, and that's so there is one to enjoy when the present becomes the past. A record underscores the memory—verifies it, even.

A certain woman was seventy-two when she died. At her funeral someone read the details of her birth recorded in joy by her mother. At the end of her life here was proof and perspective about the beginning, about the reaching and helping and brightening of her seasons. At this dying a kind of resurrection occurred, for the whole family loved their sister and each other anew. Her younger brother reading from journals on this occasion turned the hearts of the family to each other. A written line or two became their lifeline to the dry farm, the small store mother kept, the loved ones at Christmas or at daily prayer, the father's Sunday ritual, the hard times, the faithful times, the laughing times, and the inevitable struggle to add a new room as yet another baby came.

It was a wonderful, rooted remembering, that funeral. There was no shriveling sadness, but only a hearty gathering of reasons for our being and then moving on.

It seems a testimony in itself for keeping a record of the proceedings of our days.

And here is another.

The teenage son was having trouble relating to his family. His thoughts and his behavior were cluttered with the onslaught of life that came at him as fast as the inches at the end of his legs. His mother's demands especially seemed a burden. He didn't know her anymore. He wasn't sure she understood him at all, and he was shocked to discover that after all she wasn't perfect as he had thought her to be when he was much younger. His older sisters were to him mere replicas of the authority figure he resented in his mother.

Then one day he came upon his mother's open journal. Reading it was a temptation he couldn't resist. A perfunctory glance or two, almost a sneer, and then quiet as he turned the pages that revealed a spiritual side to his mother he hadn't appreciated. Soon uncomfortable tears were burning his cheeks. He learned from this irrevocable source that his mother loved him. He also realized that she prayed for him and that she was mindful of good things he had done. Then he read a note tucked inside, written by one of his sisters for Mother's Day. He'd never suspected that she was capable of such deep feeling.

He was interested in reasons she expressed for loving their mother, reasons that simply hadn't occurred to him. The warmth filling his heart opened a door in his mind. He hadn't understood. This record taught valuable lessons at the very time he needed to learn them. He gained new insights in all inter-family relating. He mellowed under the security of such a blessing and of being loved. In return, he felt love for others freshen his soul again. For him the world began all over again.

We who would give our children everything, would even sacrifice our lives for them if need be, must consider the importance of keeping records that can enrich their lives beyond description and reach them beyond our voice.

Our posterity has a right to know their roots without scrounging for them and perhaps uncovering only part. Keeping records can assure them of this. Writing our life story can help them know their parents. Knowing brings understanding, and understanding strengthens love.

We'll want to write as fine and complete a record as we can. When we keep current accounts of our lives, we should preserve these and pass them on to the next generation, as we are inspired to, with instructions that our children are to add their own histories and records. Then all the accounts should be passed on to the next generation, who are to follow the same pattern in turn.

It is the Lord's way, and it is good.

In the Bible it says, "For whatsoever things were written aforetime were written for our learning, that we through patience and comfort of the scriptures might have hope." (Romans 15:4.) This can be said of the things we write today. We build a kind of sacred supplement to the scriptures as we record our life, our testimony of Christ, our service, our struggles to learn for ourselves right and wrong.

From the land of me to the land of you is one way of describing all personal records: life stories, genealogical sheets, diaries, journals, photographic albums, and oral history tapes. What we record in our privacy can be read by posterity, in due time.

We train them in the traditions of their fathers. We keep the chain linking the generations unbroken. So, of course, will our posterity.

It's like beginning the world all over again.

How Do I Choose?

Have you ever wondered what to believe and whom to follow in the confused and polarized thinking in today's world? I have, and I recall something that's a stern reminder: "That we henceforth be no more children, tossed to and fro, and carried about with every wind of doctrine." (Ephesians 4:14.) What we need to do is learn how to discern truth from error.

An article in a newspaper revealed the dichotomy among doctors and scientists concerning some aspects of medicine and corrective or curative care. Some prescribe surgery and some, radiation. The naturalists insist we are what we eat and that nature's ways are the best. No doubt you've heard about the controversy over whether huge quantities of vitamin C will prepare the body against the cold season. Some fitness experts recommend jogging for health. Meanwhile, the podiatrists are concerned with the foot problems of the runners. Television is a good teaching aid, according to some leaders in the field of education. Other educators call it a tool of the devil and a deterrent to a child's learning processes.

Yes, there are usually at least two sides to every pet theory and at least two ways of getting where you are going. In all the onslaught of information being given us today, we need some kind of truth filter. Otherwise we'll find ourselves in the position of the proverbial centipede. Do you remember the little verse about the centipede who was happy quite until the frog, for fun, asked, " 'Pray which leg comes after which?' Which wrought his mind to such a pitch he lay distracted in the ditch, considering how to run."

How like the centipede we can be, considering how to run, how to think, what to eat, what expert to believe, what leader to follow, what choice to make! Meanwhile, life moves on, time passes, and precious opportunities are lost or serious mistakes are made as we live with indecision or follow false prophets or experiment with every new idea flung forth.

How to decide?

How to choose? How can we know truth for sure?

Some years ago in upstate New York there was a fourteen-year-old farm boy who lived in a very small community with several highly active religious groups. Each fervently tried to lure him into its congregation. His family members had split themselves up for Sunday worship, and this teenager had misgivings about the whole thing. But the preachers were pressing. One night as the boy was reading the Bible he saw this verse, "If any of you lack wisdom, let him ask of God, that giveth to all men liberally, and upbraideth not; and it shall be given him. But let him ask in faith, nothing wavering. For he that wavereth is like a wave of the sea driven with the wind and tossed." (James 1:5-6.)

So the boy went out into a secluded section of those beautiful New York woods and knelt down and talked to God about his problem: which church he should join. He had a most remarkable spiritual experience when his prayer was answered.

Maybe we aren't looking for a church. Maybe we want to know which girl to marry, or which job to take, or which house to buy, or which solution to settle upon in a specific problem. How do we choose, then?

Let's compare the whole process to music, for a moment. Rock, disco, country western, jazz, ragtime, classical, sacred, and so on. What will you listen to? How to choose? In music, the field is full for selection.

Well, in life there are countless choices too, and many voices coaxing you this way and that. Some are good for you. Some are not so good. Others are definitely bad. And with some it is hard to tell.

Choosing between kinds of music is infinitely easier than deciding which girl to marry or which job to take, let alone which church to join. At the risk of seeming simplistic, here are some simple considerations to help with the process of filtering personal truth:

1. What is the purpose of this decision; what goal are you seeking?
2. What are the facts, pro and con?
3. How can you be sure?

Let's consider the first question and go back to our example of music, for a moment. To choose music, you consider what you want it for. You check what is available, the arrangement, the price you have to pay. If your purpose is to set a mood of worship, disco music would seem a poor choice. If it's a dancing mood, the opposite is true. You are influenced by your goal.

In life you consider goals, too. What basic goal are you after in the long run in considering a decision? If it's choosing a house, you have to consider not only how attractive it is but also if you can afford it. Your goal is to live as comfortably as possible within your price range. If it's whether to be faithful to your personal values or to respond to the world's enticements, look at your life's goal again before choosing.

Getting guidance is wise. Information about music is one thing. Gathering information about your course in life is quite another. The best helpers for a life decision are parents, prophets, and the word of God, because the ramifications are eternal.

Repentance is a possibility if you make a wrong decision, but so is heartbreak. You need to give your best effort to gathering reasons for making a choice. When you've thoroughly considered all the facts, list them on paper. Remembering what the basic purpose of your decision is, you now can study the lists and choose the option that seems best.

Now, to be sure your judgment is right about music, you may want to talk it over with a trained musician. But when your life is affected, you'll want to turn to Heavenly Father in prayer for confirmation. You work it all out and present the problem before him, in faith.

Since there are so many voices around us, it seems vital that we hear his. After all, he created us.

A Woman Clothed With the Sun

May is the month to honor women—mothers, grandmothers, wives, girl graduates, helpers in the home. With women on my mind, I was impressed with a soaring thought when I read these lines from Revelation: "And there appeared a great wonder in heaven; a woman clothed with the sun." (Revelation 12:1.)

Today's woman clothed in the sun would be one wrapped in the bright things, filled with light, carrying the countenance of Christ, who is the source of all light.

There is an old and wise thought that a heroine is one who goes through the dark streets of life lighting lamps for people to see by. But the saint—the woman clothed in the sun—is herself a light, a dimension beyond the usual aspirations of a woman.

There have been such women in history, women who have been lights, who have blessed their own time as well as generations ever after. Mary, the sister of Martha, was such a woman. Mary chose the better part. She hungered and thirsted after righteousness and sat at the feet of the Master Teacher to worship, to learn the lessons of life. While Mary absorbed the light, Martha was cumbered by her much preparation and much serving. She reminds us of old Tevye's wife in *Fiddler on the Roof.* The plaintive "Do you love me?" that Tevye sings to his wife brings a response something like, "Do I love you? Haven't I shared your bed, washed your shirts, made your meals for twenty-five years?" And he, knowing full well she had done this, yet asks again with sweet hopefulness, "But, do you *love* me?"

No doubt we, too, have waited upon our men and washed their shirts and made their meals. But love? Have we only been cumbered with much serving, with too little of sitting at their feet, drawing from their wells of wisdom? Have we mothered but not truly wifed?

Esther was a woman clothed in the sun. She became queen in the place of the vain and vacillating Vashti, who refused to respond to her husband's call for her. When the king sent for Vashti to proudly show her off, she was entertaining her women friends so it wasn't convenient. And who came first? Not the king! Now lest this example come before all the women of the kingdom so that they should "despise their husbands," the king's princes demanded that Vashti be banished for one better than she. Esther was a Jewish girl who went to the king even when she wasn't bidden. She lived to do the king's will and bring him pleasure. She fasted—she and all her handmaidens. She was humble. She prepared banquets especially for him. In return, the king loved Esther more each day and gave her the desires of her heart. As a result, Esther's people, the Jews, were spared by the king from annihilation. They "rested from their enemies," the Bible says, and the month was turned from sorrow to joy and from mourning into a time of feasting and sending portions to the poor. (Esther 9:22.)

Surely the woman who touched the Savior— who connected because of her faith and purpose—was a woman clothed in the sun. He knew her touch, and she was healed while the rest of the crowds merely pressed upon him. (Matthew 9:20-22.)

Dorcas was so full of good works that the widows and neighbor women wailed at her death. Peter came, blessed her, and he presented her alive to them. (Acts 9:36-41.) She was clothed in the sun.

Elisha's Shunammite woman was such a one. She cared for his every need each time Elisha came by her home. As he promised her, she bore a child, and she searched for the prophet's blessing when the boy died. Because of her faith Elisha went to her home and raised the son from the dead. (2 Kings 4.)

Another woman who was obedient to Elisha's counsel was also filled with light or clothed in the sun. Her husband had died, and her two sons were being taken by a creditor to be bondmen. Elisha told her to gather all the empty vessels she could and fill them all from the single pot of oil she had left in her home. She did so, and the oil miraculously lasted until the last vessel was filled. Then she sold the oil, as Elisha instructed her, paid off her debts, and lived with her sons on the rest. (2 Kings 4.) Obedience sets a woman apart, fills her with light, permits her to be blessed.

Hannah vowed a vow that if God would open her womb and give her a son, she would give him back to the Lord for all the days of his life and never permit his hair to be cut. She fasted and covenanted with the Lord; he blessed her, and she bore a son whom she named Samuel. And she gave him at the temple to be a servant of God. Her prayer of thankfulness is a psalm of praise. (1 Samuel 1-2.) Surely a woman clothed in the sun would have a heart that feels gratitude.

On our own levels with our own husbands, children, mothers-in-law, neighbors, and with the Lord, we can gradually become women clothed in the sun. As we reach for Christ and his principles, as we apply the good things he has taught, we, too, can become "elect ladies," a kind of light in our own world. By us our loved ones can see the sacred things of God, his truths, his gifts. By us they'll know the rare beauties of nature. By us they can drink of the plan of life on earth, marveling at the innocence in a child's face and at the wisdom in an aged one.

If we are women clothed in the sun, reflecting the light of the Lord, our families and friends will have example, direction, and perspective to know how to judge. They can learn to know good from evil; they will understand charity and experience joy. And the brightness, the sparkle, the warmth every life needs to be satisfying can also be theirs as our loved ones are led to the Lord by women clothed in the sun.

Perspective

Winter to some is dull business at best. Skies, city snow, and barren tree trunks are the same monotonous grey. To others, winter is a season of monochromatic beauty, tone on tone across the horizon, fences, posts, and housetops. It is a unique time when one comes to know trees better, as they stand out stark in a leafless stripping against a subtle sky.

It all depends on how we look at things, doesn't it? Like the old story of the buckets my father used to tell me over and again to be certain I got the message about perspective.

There were two buckets sitting on the edge of a deep well, and one said to the other with a sigh: "This is a miserable job I have. All I do is go down and come up and go down and come up all day long. And no matter how many times I go down and come up, I always go down empty."

The other little bucket smiled and said: "That's funny. I have the same kind of a job. All I do is go down and come up and go down and come up all day long, too. But no matter how many times I go down, I always come up full."

In a world's fair, treasured art was featured in two pavilions sponsored by different religious organizations. One church exhibit included Michelangelo's haunting *Pietà*—Christ crucified, lying across the lap of grief-stricken Mary.

The other church exhibit featured Thorvaldsen's incredibly compelling *Christus*—an heroic risen Lord with his arms outstretched, revealing nail-pierced hands to the multitudes who would come unto him.

I learned a powerful lesson about perspective when on a tour of that fair and overheard a guide explain, "This first religious pavilion has the dead Christ; that one over there has the risen Savior."

Thought provoking, isn't it?

Study the work of artists through the centuries who have dealt with the same theme; the variance in perspective is evident. For example, the Nativity—Mary, Joseph, and the baby Jesus—has been rendered repeatedly by skilled and gifted painters. How different these three appear when seen through the eyes of a variety of artists! Same people, same tender theme, but interpretations vary from ornately Roman-robed and haloed figures to simply sketched suggestions of the holy family.

Now, let's talk about views of life.

Have you ever walked resolutely up the stairs or into the next room and suddenly realized that you can't recall why you are there or for what you came? The purpose of that little trip has escaped you completely, at least for the moment.

Life is like that for some of God's children all of their days. They don't ever seem to know what the trip to earth is for. Their perspective is warped. Their timing in life is off. They learn skills of social behavior after they are embarrassed. They play like they are married when they are not. Or they behave as if they are *not* when they are. They turn to their Creator only when they are in dire difficulty, instead of keeping close to him in the first place. They listen to the precepts of the world instead of saying, "Which of Heavenly Father's principles will help me now?"

Sometimes others of us may stop during periods of pressure and find ourselves at the top of the stairs, so to speak, momentarily at a loss for understanding, but the difference is that we know where we can turn for help, for perspective, for principles.

Here's another example. What if a football player walked into the stadium dressed in tennis shorts, wielding a hockey stick, insisting on playing the game by baseball regulations? What kind of inappropriate behavior would that be? What would be the outcome?

The wrong perspective makes poor preparation for performance.

Yet sometimes we handle our precious lives, our one chance to live on earth, in just such confusion. But there is no need for us to be like the mythical mixed-up athlete. The gospel of Jesus Christ in its fullness gives us the eternal perspective of who we are and why we are here and how life is to be lived in order to reap the richest reward.

Yes, the right perspective makes all the difference.

A friend of mine was stricken with polio during those terrible years before the Salk vaccine. She was a young mother and a gifted actress living in the East, surrounded by people whose professional pursuits colored their perspective of life. When the tragedy hit my friend, she was hospitalized for weeks along with others who had been similarly stricken. The trauma of paralysis and breathing problems, of dealing with therapy and coping with a variety of reactions to the situation was demanding of the best in everybody.

My friend watched people grow or flounder, complain or try to help, depending upon what their perspective was, what they understood about life and trials and hope. Suddenly she valued her childhood training of deeply significant religious principles. Life was but a moment in the eternal scheme of things; and it wasn't what happened to you—it was what you did about it; and you don't sacrifice the important things for lesser ones. All the memories of good training from loving parents filled her heart and her life, really, in those days of confinement. At last she was able to reach out and teach others the secret of hanging on, of looking on the bright side, of turning to Heavenly Father for understanding and comfort as well as direction.

The day came when my friend was well in body

and stronger than ever in her heart and soul about what counts in life. She gives thanks for the beautiful truths she's learned from terrible trouble. What perspective!

See, it's all in the way we look at things—all in the way we deal with them.

Our personal worth, our essence of human dignity, is not so much in what we accomplish as in what we understand. For proof of this we need only to look at the troubled, hopeless lives around us of people who do not know the Lord and his principles, who do not have the proper perspective of the purpose of life and the goal of eternity.

But we do. And if we'll live as if we do, then when we get to the top of the stairs—those proverbial golden stairs *this* time—we'll know why we are there and all the promises of God will be fulfilled for us. I know this.

Free Agency

In one of America's national forest reserve areas there is an underground tunnel that is not only deep and narrow, it seems endlessly long. One must crawl on hands and knees through this rocky, pitch black confinement with a flashlight tied about the neck to light the way. The reward for this challenging activity is a spectacular view of valleys and rivers and farmland patterns below the mountain from which one emerges. Nonetheless, it is an adventure a person usually has no intention of repeating.

When we took this trek, something occurred that also had happened when we made our scrunched-up shuffle through a black tunnel in one of the pyramids in Egypt. Part way through, a voice cried out in the dark: "Hey, I want to go back. I want out!" The answer was ever the same: "Keep moving. There *is* no turning back." It is like the old adage "The way in is easy, but the way out is hard" or "When one picks up one end of the stick, one picks up the other."

Isn't life like that? Sometimes we find ourselves in situations that we slipped into easily; they have become uncomfortable to us but cannot easily be turned from: certain relationships we've made, habits we've formed, lies we've told, directions we've taken, life-styles we've cultivated, weight we've added, or attitudes we've developed.

Yes, the way in is easy; but, oh, the way out is often hard! Guilt and agony, frustrations and pain, may be avoided by considering what's ahead.

The greatest gift God has given his children is life. One of the most valued aspects of this experience is our free agency, our innate right to choose. Parents have striven against children; men have died as martyrs for the cause of choice to worship as they pleased; nations have rallied in the pursuit of liberty; battles have been fought in preserving independence.

Our personal independence, our right to make choices, is precious. Circumstances can be thrust upon us, but we still have our option of how we will respond to them, how we will act or react. We can largely determine what course we'll take. This is the life of life. Now, how much pain we have along the way is often dependent upon our personal preparation, our understanding of what comes after choice. Where will this choice take us? What principles will work in this situation? What rules govern the action? What means to what end? What is down the tunnel?

Speaking of the mountainous tunnel we scrambled through, we recall that some people came prepared with burlap bags to strap around their knees as buffers against cold, damp, rough terrain. Others of us just endured to the end, miserable as we inched along.

Though learning through personal experience is a much praised principle in some circles, our trip through the dark tunnel would have been far more endurable and the view at the end just as breathtaking if we had come prepared with burlap bags to protect our knees. So it is in life, really. Though we are free souls and can choose any course we like, learning from the experience of others can save us a lot of pain. We can learn from both positive and negative examples. But for each generation to reinvent the wheel, to find that a candle flame is hot by touching, seems foolish indeed. It is time-wasting and life-limiting for every one of us to struggle through every tunnel, figure every equation, question every protecting principle. It seems wiser to quit shadowboxing with fundamentals, quit muddling through to claim our own rules, quit insisting upon learning *only* by personal experience.

The foreword of a wonderful old book titled *Light From Many Lamps* contains this statement by Thomas Macaulay: "Every generation can enjoy the use of a vast hoard bequeathed to it by antiquity and transmits that hoard, augmented by fresh acquisitions, to future ages."

This is true in science, literature, and scholarship of all kinds. If only it were true in personal relationships and individual decision-making! Unfailingly, in each generation, even the Ten Commandments are challenged afresh, the same mistakes are made, the same sins committed with inevitable accompanying misery. Yet this need not be so. Those who do avoid personal pitfalls by observing the mistakes of others are most apt to keep free from pain. And in a world full of incredible challenges and personal pressures, the record of what has gone before in the area of human experience could be as valuable to us as anything we could consider. The consequences of choices made by people in the past is a valid record of what consequences will occur from those same choices made today. The Bible is a history of people making choices and what happened because of those choices. The daily press gives perspective on this, too. Revenge and retaliation did not breed love between people in Christ's day. Neither will they breed love today. Problems have not been solved by anger and killing in the past. Nor will they be likely to in the future.

Freedom to reason, freedom to choose, to pick up the stick or crawl through the tunnel, is still man's most precious option. But we suggest that consideration of which stick or how to maneuver through the tunnel is important. There seldom has been a time more pressing than today when the tried and tested and, we might add, eternal principles of the past were needed to give perspective to people as they struggle to build a firm and fine society with strong, happy families of stable people.

In Proverbs we read, "Ponder the path of thy feet, and let all thy ways be established." (Proverbs 4:2, 6.) This statement sums up a brief, beautiful chapter of excellent counsel that includes the idea that one should get wisdom and also

understanding. And the sooner the better! Just because some
people crawl through the tunnel without the benefit of burlap
doesn't preclude the fact that there may be a better way to see a
view of farmlands. It just may be wiser yet to skip the tunnel al-
together.

We need wisdom to use our free agency for our
own best benefit. With that wisdom, if we get understanding
also, we will realize another important dimension—that just
because many people are crawling through the tunnel as a means
to a certain end, doesn't mean we have to. In other words, just
because some people wear a particular style of clothing, follow a
certain diet, experiment with an alternate life-style doesn't mean
that such behavior or choices are good for us.

Since we are into life, however, and there is no
way of getting out of it short of dishonorable death, it helps if we
learn from others, consider past performances and match the
wisdom of the ages with the counsel of God. And then make our
free choice.

The hymn "Know This, That Every Soul Is Free"
has an appropriate message for each of us:

> Know this, that every soul is free
> To choose his life and what he'll be;
> For this eternal truth is given,
> That God will force no man to heav'n.
>
> He'll call, persuade, direct aright,
> And bless with wisdom, love, and light,
> In nameless ways be good and kind,
> But never force the human mind.
>
> May we no more our powers abuse,
> But ways of truth and goodness choose;
> Our God is pleased when we improve
> His grace and seek his perfect love.

People and Problems

It is a changing world. But that isn't a new situation. It's been a changing world since Eve tangled with the serpent and Adam tangled with Eve. What may be different is the way we dress and the kind of transportation we've invented for ourselves. But challenges, temptations, relationships, and rules don't change. And neither does God.

Questioning looks are being cast at time-honored traditions. Old values are being reconsidered. New ones are being experimented with, and some foolish detours taken in the process. Yet there is something healthy about today's seeking populace—young and old, professional and lay person. Bosses are employing experts to help them with personnel problems. Big companies are hiring staff psychologists for counseling. Happy workers are better workers, they're discovering. Teachers are going back to school themselves to learn how to get the slow learner to move along, how to cope with the emotionally disturbed and the physically or spiritually deprived in their classes. They're learning, too, ways of challenging the brightest person in class.

Psychologists conduct endless studies today to increase their understanding of people. They have now begun to define what has long been suspected by families, churches, societies, businesses, governments, and educational institutions: that the problems of life are "people problems." One educator said, "I got my degree in institutional administration; and now that I'm working, I find my problems aren't really institutional: they're people oriented."

It seems clear that there are at least two categories into which we humans can be lumped. There are problem people and people with problems.

Society is only as tolerable, delightful, or successful as the people in it. By society we mean any association of human beings—from a family to an incorporated township. It is hoped that we number ourselves among the wise people who recognize their problems and who seek perspective for solutions or for coping, or for enduring with grace, if it comes to that.

One thing we can be sure of: neither here nor hereafter are we suddenly going to emerge with qualities we haven't developed and a pattern of life to which we aren't suited. It is important for us to do something about the things we can change and to accept with a certain equanimity and tolerance those things we can't.

No amount of legislation, arbitration, or organization will help the individual who has low self-esteem or scant appreciation of where he or she fits into the whole big world with its numberless masses. The same might be said of the arrogant, self-seeking soul who aggressively takes over any scene but misses the mellowing that an understanding and helpful attitude can provide. Christ was strong. But Christ related to simple men as well as great ones. He lifted the loser and took time for the stricken. He helped people with problems. And he loved problem people, though he disapproved of their sins.

Life today would be sweeter and more fulfilling for all if there were more Christlike people in our lives.

The best method for our working on society's number one challenge of problem people and people with problems is to return again to the ultimate success manual and the perfect model for us: the word of God for the text, our Savior himself as model, as proof of practicing what has been preached. A study of the life of Jesus gives us more than a record of his verbal teachings; it gives us a powerful portrait of a living man. We know that Jesus Christ came into the world to atone for the sins of man. What we often forget is that he came to set a standard of personal behavior for us that, if followed, would bring people to such perfection that they would dwell together in peace and joy. It would be heaven. Only if every one of us lives as Christ did will it ever be a pleasant and problem-free society. Anything less than that wouldn't be worth going through for-ever and ever, now would it?

We, at least, can start the ball rolling in the right way. We can start living after the manner of Christ, after the manner of happiness.

The world is changing. We need to change, too, in all the appropriate ways. God's standards don't change, of course. His principles for us to live by are eternal—they were guides for earliest mankind and are found to be roots for the choice philosophies of all men in the great cultures of history before the time of Christ and down the ages since then.

Taking a fresh look at doing something about ourselves seems a momentous task at times. There is a simple story, oft-quoted, which delights me because it so clearly points up a truth about the behavior patterns of mankind.

When a newlywed served baked ham to her husband, he noticed she had cut the ends off and asked why. "That's the way mother always did it," she replied with a shrug.

When his mother-in-law came for a visit, he asked her the same question. "That's the way my mother did it," she replied.

Finally, he asked his wife's grandmother, who answered, "That's the only way I could get it into the pan."

So, whether it is how we bake ham, celebrate summer, discipline children, show love, or worship God, let's take another look. Why not consider if we are people persisting in problems we could well solve and be rid of. And more cour-ageously, maybe we are problem people who make the world miserable for others by persisting in doing things as they always have been done. The way we bake a ham may not be all that cataclysmic to someone else, but the way we deal with trouble and the way we relate to our neighbors might.

The Bible—What's in It for Me?

Sometimes writers write to please themselves. Their books are simply something they want to say. Other materials are prepared with the needs of the reader in mind—assuming the reader is a seeking, growing person, concerned with what it means to be human today and with a certain self-appreciation plus a hearty hope for a place in God's plan for his children. The scriptures form such a book.

We've heard people say, "The Bible? Why read it? What's in it for me?"

You'll get honest answers and help from this inspired source. You'll find reasons for giving up the procrastination game. You'll want to stop existing and start living. You'll find some specific how-to-do information to make the ideal real; not just nice, philosophical thoughts on being good and qualifying for the highest heaven.

You'll find various collections of readables to stir up your thought processes, stretch your mind in new directions; they'll give you something to brighten your conversation with, too, when talk of the weather or ball game scores runs out.

You'll get perspective on communicating with others and with God. You'll learn what is right and wrong, and why.

There are even discussions and pointers about becoming a prepared leader and a contented, contributing follower. It takes both kinds to make a great world or a good group gather; and everybody has a turn at each role.

With all the answers to the really important questions contained in the scriptures, you'll get special and specific help in how to find which of Heavenly Father's principles will help you when. You'll find a yardstick for measuring truth and sure-fire ways to come up with the right decision. Options and alternatives at your fingertips will help you live in the world but stay clear of its damaging entanglements.

Each of us is responsible for his own happiness and salvation, too. We needn't be at the mercy of our heredity or our environment or even our cultural boundaries. We can do better with what we have to work with, and we can change what we want to if we want to badly enough and if we have the right kind of information to act upon.

Though our special circumstances suggest that we all ought to be winners in life, it takes some tall thinking and some inimitable insight to lend us proper perspective.

God's word can give us that. Life is his plan. It is his system to help us grow and to see if we'll be faithful and valiant all the way. He set up the rules and gave us the guidelines. To get right answers, we have to search the scriptures with help from experienced people who are inspired by God and who keep in very close contact with Heavenly Father.

But talk about a generation gap, some might exclaim! What could a person who lived two thousand years ago possibly say that could be helpful to us, the twentieth-century generation?

And we firmly answer, everything.

The Lord has all the answers to all the questions, to all the problems, you tangle with each day. He is the basic source, the ultimate authority, for all that ever has been written about human relations, communication, popularity, success, and peace of mind. Under the direction of God, the Eternal Father, Christ was the Creator. He is also our Savior. He knows whereof he speaks.

Listen to what he says:

Service: Let your light so shine before
                men, that they may see your good
                works, and glorify your Father
                which is in heaven (Matthew
                5:16).

Others: Whatsoever ye would that men
                should do to you, do ye even so to
                them (Matthew 7:12).

Success: Seek ye first the kingdom of God,
                and his righteousness; and all
                these things shall be added unto
                you (Matthew 6:33).

Humility: When thou doest alms, let not thy
                left hand know what thy right
                hand doeth (Matthew 6:3).

Sincerity: But thou, when thou prayest,
                enter into thy closet, and when
                thou hast shut thy door, pray to
                thy Father which is in secret; and
                thy Father which seeth in secret
                shall reward thee openly (Mat-
                thew 6:6).

Forgiveness: Love your enemies, bless them
                that curse you, do good to them
                that hate you, and pray for them
                which despitefully use you, and
                persecute you (Matthew 5:44).

Spiritual   Watch and pray always, lest ye be
Strength: tempted by the devil, and ye be
                led away captive by him (3 Nephi
                18:15).

There is one last thought that I would like to share with you about the matter of finding in the scriptures the answers and directions to all aspects of life, and that is this statement from the Savior:

"Behold I have given unto you my gospel, and this is the gospel which I have given unto you—that I came into the world to do the will of my Father, because my Father sent me . . . therefore, according to the power of the Father I will draw all men unto me.

"Therefore, what manner of men ought ye to be? Verily I say unto you, even as I am." (3 Nephi 27:13-15, 27.)

I am convinced that the scriptures, the word of God, can help us become even as he is.

Wintry Day

March is a tumultuous month, isn't it? It has a way of stirring up our thoughts like billowing fog banks clouding over mountains and skyscrapers and wind-bent juniper alike. But that isn't all bad. In fact, at this season there is so much that is good about being stirred up inside—to think again in restless searching for personal position. We might ask ourselves such questions as: "Where am I now?" "What notion am I clinging to?" "What wisdom has come out of trial?" "What exciting supposition has surfaced from today's media?" "What should I do about the sweet feelings deep inside that trail peace and comfort but seem unreachable?"

On such a March day I stood at Peggy's Cove in Nova Scotia, where winter leaves last. It was the time of the water birds, when only the cry of the crane was company for me. The ocean was angry and broke wildly over jutting rocks, and the swift undertow regularly swept clean the stretch of beach below me. The gulls, with heaven on their wings, dipped and soared in matching rhythm to the relentless sea.

Relentlessly the ebb and the flow, the crash and the sweep, the cries and the silence, marked life's pattern for me once more—all the comings and goings in life, the births and the deaths, the filled times and empty hours, the joyful crowdings and the silent apartness. I was one of God's children, counted numerous as the sands I stood on; and I wondered at his capacity to love and know each of us when we struggle so to know only ourselves.

I wondered at the ceaseless sea, whether war or

peace, earthquake or quiet, dry season or flood, wickedness in hidden places or church bells tolling, the breakers' crash and retreat to gather force again. Relentlessly, too, day follows night. The seasons are the same. As winter's end signals spring's beginning, it seems a good time to sense the miracle that is our life, modeled for us in nature.

Each of us must finally take time to consider the point beyond which we will not go, the ideals by which we are directed and the idealists to whom we are indebted, and to identify the true source of strength as well as a cause of weakness. We must look to our lives.

I think of Ann Morrow Lindberg and her retreat to the sea to study her life through the symbol of shells. And Thoreau who took his solitude because he wished to live deliberately and "front only the essential facts of life, and see if I could not learn," as he wrote, "what it had to teach, and not, when I came to die, discover that I had not lived."

Now, at the season of equinox, of seasonal change, of the dry branch and then the green, of frozen ground giving way to puddles, of days lengthening, of death and life again, let us talk about our adventure on earth as witnessed in the lives of others. Perhaps the tempering of such a time as this will be as helpful to you as it has been to me.

We have a little loved one in Seattle where the daily rain keeps sun and stars alike hidden much of the time, so she hadn't really seen stars. We think there is magic in stargazing and lessons to learn from them—they are brighter in winter's night, you know. I explained this to this little girl when we stood one clear night looking into heaven. I smiled at her wonderment at first seeing stars crowd the nighttime.

"Are they there every time it gets dark, even if I can't see them?" she asked. I assured her they were, even behind the rain clouds.

"Then darkness isn't so bad, is it, if you know the stars are there."

It has its application to life, doesn't it?

Leslie R. Smith said that if we'd learn to look at stars instead of into dark corners, darkness would always be beautiful. "Stars," he wrote, "tell us that night is the most joyous part of the day. It is the time of homecoming after a hard day's work . . . we step into the boundless love of home and family. Night is the time for rest and for sleep. So it is with death. It is life's night. It is a glorious homecoming. It is a reunion with those who have gone before. It is rest from labor. It is simply to lie back in the Everlasting Arms."

Ebb tide, high tide, of winter into spring, of death into life, it seems suitable to share one stanza, at least, from Orson F. Whitney's hymn, "The Wintry Day Descending to Its Close":

> The wintry day, descending to its close,
> Invites all wearied nature to repose,
> And shades of night are falling dense and fast
> Like sable curtains closing o'er the past.
> Pale through the gloom the newly fallen snow
> Wraps in a shroud the silent earth below
> As though 'twere mercy's hand had spread the pall
> A symbol of forgiveness unto all.

And on this note, may every season be a joy to you.

Remembering

Beauty

Helen Keller was an amazing woman with uncommon gifts. She couldn't hear or see, and she learned to speak laboriously; but what a marvelous spirit she had! I met her years ago as she visited the sick in a veteran's hospital and lifted their spirits because her own was on higher ground. Being in her presence was a beautiful experience. I remember her saying something which has long since been put into print and which deeply affected my life:

"I who am blind can give one hint to those who see. Use your eyes as if tomorrow you would be stricken blind. And the same method can be applied to the other senses. Hear the music of voices, the song of a bird, the mighty strains of an orchestra, as if you would be stricken deaf tomorrow. Touch each object as if tomorrow your tactile sense would fail. Smell the perfume of flowers, taste with relish each morsel, as if tomorrow you could never smell and taste again. Make the most of every sense, glory and beauty which the world in all the facets of pleasure reveals to you through the several means of contact which nature provides. But of all the senses, I am sure that sight is the most delightful."

Miss Keller overcame obstacles of the most extreme kind. And, in the process, touched others. Many people with less physical challenge also have brought beauty into the lives of others. You no doubt know people who, because of their in-tuneness with God, their goodness to their fellowmen, their brightness about daily grind, their willingness to live above trifling things—who through their gift to see beauty in everything, lift the sights of others.

My husband was given a church assignment to work closely with a man whom we hadn't known before. A few weeks passed, and I saw the man in the foyer of the meeting hall and asked him when I'd be able to meet his wife. I didn't even know what she looked like, and I was anxious to strike a relationship with her.

"Oh, go meet her now, why don't you?" he encouraged. "She's in the multipurpose room. Just introduce yourself to her."

"How will I know her?" I asked.

"Easy," he replied. "She's the most beautiful woman in there. You can't miss her, really." Then he went on to wax eloquent, as the saying goes, about this gorgeous creature who was his wife.

I moved on into the multipurpose room and looked for a woman who was a cross between a movie queen and an angel from on high. I saw many mothers with children flocking about. I saw young women abloom with expected babies. I saw old women bent over a quilting frame, and middle-age contributors who were cumbered with much serving. Fine-looking women. Good women, too, all. But as for something akin to the most beautiful woman in the world, there was not.

I asked some of the women I knew if they could point out this man's wife. They did, and I walked over to introduce myself; but, frankly, I was startled into silence. This woman had little going for her in the sense of classic beauty. Her eyes were unusually wide set. Her nose featured big nostrils clearly visible below an oversized hump on the bridge. Her teeth were badly bucked and she smiled broadly, dropping her chin into her neck in the process. I wondered what cruel joke he had played on me?

But then the woman spoke to me, first, while I was collecting my wits. And that's where true beauty and goodness in a spirit worked its magic on the beholder. In moments I was under her spell. She was the kind of person who looked you right in the eye with an "I'm delighted to be with you" kind of attitude. Later on it was she who baked two dozen apple pies for the church fund-raising bake sale. Not once, you must understand, but three times a week until their apple tree was picked clean. I can see her now, walking the block with her children, pulling the little red wagon full of applie pies to deliver the orders. And if someone was ill, they got a pie and a cheery note —free!

To this day I look at her as a beautiful woman. I have thought back on that first meeting and wondered at my initial shock at her appearance. Oh, her nose hasn't changed, nor her teeth, and so on; but on her, they look great! Do you understand? I see her now with my eyes quickened by my heart. She does this to people. Her husband was absolutely right. She is a most exquisite human being.

Helen Keller's suggestion that we start using our all to view the world around us is like seeing things with eyes quickened by our hearts. Remember what Duke Senior said in Shakespeare's "As You Like It"?

> And this our life, exempt from public haunt,
> Finds tongues in trees, books in the running brooks,
> Sermons in stones, and good in every thing.

Let me suggest that there is beauty in all the places one would expect—in Wordsworth's host of daffodils, in Masefield's sea, in Emerson's sunsets and Thoreau's winter animals, in Willa Cather's plains, in all the orderly arrangements of nature and God's universe—there is a certain magnitude in even the smallest part. But when it's found in God's ultimate creation, a child of God of whatever age or whatever facial structure, there is true beauty just a little lower than the angels, as the scriptures tell us.

There is beauty all around, and he who has the eyes for it shall see.

Records

The story is told of the visitor to a big city zoo who was startled to see the huge gorilla in his cage, sitting upon his captive zoo keeper and reading Charles Darwin's *Origin of the Species*. The gorilla was heard to muse, "Now, am I my keeper's brother or am I my brother's keeper?"

That animal's situation is not so different from ours. We, too, are intensely curious about who we are, what we are, where we come from, and why we are here on earth. Keeping records and passing them from generation to generation fits us into our place with ancestors and descendants and gives important continuity to a fleeting life.

Our family have always been avid record keepers. We encouraged our children to keep journals, and at first this project was received in the same mood as the proverbial Saturday night bath—they did it whether they liked it or not. But it worked. These children have turned into parents and are insisting upon record-keeping with their own children. Until a child can write, an adult is scribe. At a family reunion we learned some revealing things about our posterity as we scanned the entries in these precious childish records. Five-year-old Annie's startling one-liner was, "Today I sat on my goldfish. It squashed!"

Four-year-old Jake's entry included the complaint about long church services on the Sabbath. It said, "I hate Sundays. I wish they were in a foreign country."

With all of this record-keeping, everybody knows how old everybody else is. I wasn't really surprised, then, to read in one of the other's record, "I won't ask grandmother to play ball at the picnics anymore. She's nearly a hundred."

Personal records offer a precious perspective.

Here are some excerpts from records of people you might have heard of:

Anne Frank, the little Jewish girl, kept a diary while she and her family were in hiding during the World War II Nazi occupation of Holland. She wrote: "It's an odd idea for someone like me to keep a diary . . . who would be interested in the unbosomings of a thirteen-year-old school girl. Still, what does that matter, the reason for my starting a diary is that I have no real friend."

Leonard Read, President of the Foundation for Economic Education, Inc., and author of several books, wrote: "I made a resolution to keep a daily journal into which I would write any good ideas given me by others or any that I might come upon by myself. It will be eighteen years next month, and I haven't missed a day. At first this was extremely difficult, but within a year or two it became a joy."

Daphne du Maurier has published a notebook which includes some personal perspectives and a most touching account of her feelings about the death of her beloved husband —death as described numerous times in her past novels was far different from death experienced. This is a fascinating and help-ful account to read. She is an incredibly sensitive and strong woman.

And then there is Anna Greenwood, out in the Rockies, who is a hundred and four years old and still keeps a personal record so that her "trained brain and hands won't rust away," as she says. She fills it with personal philosophies such as, "Idleness breeds discontentment," and "Unhappiness is bad for the health." And the clinching counsel, "Don't think of the gray in your hair. Think of the fun you had in putting it there."

Part of record keeping is the gathering of family information and the locating of our ancestors. Several years ago I took our college-age son on a trip with me to Chicago. I had work to do. He is our born-to-the-cause genealogist and had traced an obituary item through to locate the grave in a Chicago cemetery. But he wasn't sure, and he couldn't get a confirmation from the public records people in that big city. So he went to Chicago, and he tramped around the cemeteries and shuffled through record departments until finally he located the cemetery plot where everything meshed. We went there and with the sexton's permission put up a sign that said, "Anybody who visits this cemetery plot, please contact Elaine Cannon at such and such a phone number."

That was Thursday. Tuesday I arrived home, and there was a message about a call from Chicago. My grandfather, dead now for over a hundred years, did have a brother buried in Chicago and relatives did visit his grave that weekend. A first cousin to my father had few relatives until that Sunday when she visited her father's grave and responded to our note. She hadn't known we existed. We had known nothing of her or her loved ones. Now she has many cousins and caring family members. Record keeping is dramatic, healing work. It is a work of the heart.

There is one other aspect to it. Like millions of other people, I watched *Roots* on television. I remember in one sequence where baby Kizzy is taken to the mountain top by her father and presented before God with the statement, "Here is the only thing bigger than you are, Kizzy—the universe." I thrilled again at that scene. I thrilled when I read it in Alex Haley's stirring book. I see similarity in it to the custom in our own family of my husband's taking each of our babies in turn in his arms to give him or her a name and a father's blessing. I have records of these blessings—recorded in our family files just as the blessings of Jacob to his sons are recorded in the Bible.

Our record-keeping, record-studying, record-researching, and record-sharing teach us that we are not so different, we children of God. We can learn from each other about misery and joy, about adventure and learning and enduring, and about how families feel about each other. Oh, this activity not only binds the hearts of the children to their fathers, I believe it binds us children—mankind—to our Heavenly Father, who is one and the same for all of us.

Exercise in Joy

It is the season of Thanksgiving, and a welcome time it is. How healing is our custom of feasting because of our plenty and of counting our blessings because we have so many! Think for a moment, if you will, about some special things you're grateful for.

We do have a lot to be thankful for, don't we? There is much to warm our hearts and bring patience and appreciation into our relationships. There is much to move us to bow before the Lord in a real unfolding of our souls. How rich are our gifts! How precious even the smallest comfort is that comes to us through our Heavenly Father! For those of us who are dependent upon a God we know and love, it becomes very clear to us that one of our best blessings is the knowledge that he lives and cares about us, is mindful of the details of our lives, and is privy to our problems. This is increasingly evident as we see people in the world struggle with their lives because they don't know where to get answers; they are without a support system. Or they simply have given in to self-pity instead of blessing-counting.

I have a wonderful friend who has taught me many kinds of lessons, in the way good friends can. She practices what she calls "an exercise in joy" each morning of her life. When you understand some of the details of her life, you wonder what she has to be joyous about. She's lived alone since her illness crippled her thirty-five years ago. She's practically helpless in the usual sense of the term. She's a wheelchair person with a list of ailments serious enough to conquer the most spirited person.

She moves awkwardly and in pain. Besides being paralyzed, trying to grip anything from a fork to a washcloth adds to her suffering. For her, even to breathe is risky business. She lives on social security and the generosity of the neighbors, with special household help coming from a remarkable group of youth who like to be around her so much that they drop in to help with the house, run errands, and water plants.

Polio left her a physical lump in a wheelchair, but spiritually she soars. She doesn't just endure, nor has she merely survived. She has lived. She has learned what life is for and what comes next and how God works. This perspective allows her to awaken each morning and conduct her "exercise in joy," her ritual of thanksgiving.

This is simply a blessing-counting time when she thanks God for life—one more day of life—in which to learn. She thanks him for eyes to see the sky from her window; for ears to hear the morning bird; she moves on down her body and soul and recites the gratefulness she feels for taste buds, for a sense of smell, for touch to feel textured petals and fabric weaves, for soft yarn and slick surfaces like fine porcelain. She expresses appreciation for the folks who help, including the anonymous friend who invented wheelchairs and motors that work them, and the maintenance man who comes to replace the battery upon which her mobility depends. At last she gives a tearful thanks for the truths she learned through terrible trouble. She has come to know God. She has come to understand that life is school; it isn't fulfillment. Life is learning, and heaven comes later. Life is an adventure, a glorious adventure, and it is to be lived. She'd never have known these particular things without her special kind of trouble. And she thanks God for this. And I thank God for her.

There are some other things I am thankful for; and as I mention one or two of them, maybe they will trigger your own thinking about your blessings, and you can conduct your own personal exercise in joy during the Thanksgiving season.

I am thankful today for people like the woman I have just mentioned and the debt I owe them for luster as well as lessons in life.

I am thankful for my knowledge that God lives. There is overwhelming evidence of this in my personal life, in my public work, in the reports I've gathered of other people's experiences with a loving Heavenly Father who cares about the details. I am thankful for his gospel, aren't you, really? What would you do if you didn't know that the plan of life is his, and that our very lives are a gift from him? He means it when he says, "If any of you lack wisdom, let him ask of God, that giveth to all men liberally, and upbraideth not; and it shall be given him." (James 1:5.)

This is a beautiful blessing to be thankful for, and it is one all mankind can share in if they but will. I am thankful for saving principles—saving because when we live by them instead of by the ways of the world, we get along better with each other. We not only get along better with each other, we have a wonderful time together. Consider with me for a moment such a marvelous doctrine hidden in familiar phrases: "All that I have I will give unto thee"; "A soft answer turneth away wrath"; "Thy sins are forgiven thee"; "Love your enemies"; "From him that would borrow of thee turn not thou away"; "Blessed are they that mourn: for they shall be comforted"; "Agree with thine adversary quickly"; "When thou prayest enter into thy closet . . . and thy Father which seeth in secret shall reward thee openly"; "Take my yoke upon you and learn of me . . . and ye shall find rest for your souls."

We have, my friends, so much to help us and so much to enrich us.

I know a very special little boy whose mother died when he was three years old. Shortly after the funeral his father had gathered the three little ones about him and was trying to help them to understand that God lived and he did love them even though their mommy had died. This father used as proof of God's love the wonders that they could see about them. He described autumn leaves, harvest foods, migrating birds, nut-gathering squirrels at their summer place, and the first snow crowning the high peaks beyond their home. One evening as he was explaining all of this, the father suddenly became aware that he had a captive audience. The boys were listening. He said to them, "Come on, let's go out into God's world and see all of this for ourselves." They all ran for their warm clothing, hurried out to the car, and then had to wait for the three-year-old, who couldn't seem to find his boots to wade through mountain snow in. But soon he came bursting out of the door, threw his arms up into the air, and cried, "Oh, hello, Heavenly Father. And thanks a million."

Well, that is a great way to feel—all of our troubles and disappointments notwithstanding, thanks a million!

We can talk turkey and the gathering of the clan, we can wrestle with the little ones, enjoy football, and make a day of it. All of this is only self-indulgence, however, if we partake of the pleasures without remembrance of the Giver.

I guess what we need to do is work our own exercise of joy. Thanksgiving is a good time for thoughtful consideration of all that we do have. It is a fine time to start.

Eight Ways to Preserve Freedom

Did your mother ever read to you the story of Hans, the little Dutch boy of long, long ago? He put his finger in the dike to plug the leak and held it there for hours until someone finally came along to help? Hans was a special kind of hero who single-handedly saved his city from flooding. My mother used to tell that story to me, and it filled my heart and mind with the wonder of people who did brave and good deeds, who thought of the good of others instead of the comfort or safety of self.

I have never looked upon the dikes of Holland as I've visited that fair country without remembering little Hans and feeling a certain surge that all round us are things we could do to lift mankind and preserve the good life.

Chief Justice George Sutherland said that the saddest epitaph which can be carved in the memory of a vanished liberty is that it was lost because its possessors failed to stretch forth a saving hand while yet there was time.

If each of us stretched forth a hand, if each strengthened his or her will, if each stirred up thoughts aimed toward doing some simple or great good, if each counted the blessings of freedom and liberty, perhaps we could be a kind of Hans in our own day, in our own country, in our own family.

Start now to preserve the precious freedom that is yours today. You may not be a political leader, but you can wield an important influence in the cause of freedom. In your own world, in your own way, you can toss into a pond an important pebble that finally will affect the lives of innumerable people for good. The pace you set, the people you involve, and the attitudes you stimulate will create ripples that will spread and reach and effectively touch and finally make an important difference in the preservation of the liberty we love.

Don't wait for someone else to start.

Don't expect some other person to get on with it.

Stretch forth your own hand. Put forth your own effort. Guarantee freedom for your future while yet there is time. Here are eight ways:

1. *Talk about it.* Talk about it all the time. Blessing-count about freedom out loud among your friends and family. Talk about freedom on the bus, during dates, eating lunch. Make your own personal collection of quotable quotes on the subject. Memorize some. Use the topic for the next brief talk in front of an audience at church or school. Lead a family discussion about this important principle.

2. *Sing about it.* Sing the songs of independence, of freedom, of nobility in service to one's country, of love of country and its flag. Sing about freedom around the campfire, at pep assemblies, during conventions, on programs, and during family reunions. From all the music there is, choose some that speaks of freedom. The more we hear about it, the more we'll value our liberty to live, choose, act, and grow in such a climate. Folk songs, anthems, patriotic tunes make you conscious of your country in a very special way.

3. *Write about it.* Write about freedom and the blessings of liberty in your personal journal, in your company or club newsletter, in your church bulletin. Get statements from peers, civic leaders, faculty or family members. Invite guest writers to suggest what freedom means to them. In a family or at work or church or in a social setting, give an award that is deliberately established and prepared by you. Maybe your award will be to the "Freedom Fan of the Year" or to the "Freedom Family" of the month. You decide, but remember to write down the

name of the citation and the reason why that person or those persons are winning this particular award in the cause of preserving freedom. Make the presentation of the award a special occasion.

4. *Read about it.* History is fascinating, isn't it, if you have a purpose in mind for reading about it? You can do a brushup on your country's preservation of a free land where people can grow and families can flourish and God can be worshipped without restrictions. Make it a family or friendly project to collect pictures, stories, slogans, and sayings about freedom. When you are informed, you are more effective.

5. *Promote it.* Stage your own private Freedom Week. This could happen with your church group or your school club, your family association or your neighborhood. Each day could feature a different event. Everyone might dress in flag colors on the same day. Houses or halls could be decked with bunting and flags. A historical movie could be shown; a freedom seminar held; a poetry, essay, or oratory contest staged; a pageant presented, with participants depicting famous historical freedom fighters or incidents from history that gave us liberty. Prizes ought to be flag kits or flag cakes or flag posts or flags to fly if there is a contest of some kind conducted.

6. *Parade it.* Since everyone loves a parade, and a parade really knows no age barriers, a town or neighborhood parade, a school or camp or church parade, proves to be a great way to get everyone thinking about liberty and love of land to stir up people to wanting to live to preserve their freedom. Have on hand a lot of blue ribbons to award age group, topic, and creative ability prizes for those participating in a formal parade or a simple garage exhibit.

7. *Have a ball.* Stage a freedom fancy. George Washington, Benjamin Franklin, and presidents of our day have held balls. Go all out for a ball of your own. Make the atmosphere colonial for your next prom, girls' dance, club social, or family reunion. Everything from powdered wigs and ruffled shirts

on the punch pourers and entertainers to a "minuet contest" will add spice to the spree.

8. *Make freedom a fad.* Wave the flag on every appropriate occasion, including when a guest comes to visit your home. Be a committee of one to interest your neighbors in flag flying. Brush up on flag rules, regulations, and etiquette. Stand, salute, and applaud with gusto when you are supposed to honor the flag.

These are ideas. Surely you'll come up with some better ones of your own. The important thing is to get excited about what we have in a land of the free and home of the brave. Never let it be said of us that a vanished liberty happened because we failed to stretch forth a saving hand as little Hans of Holland did.

Easter

Easter is a most sacred holiday. It is, in fact, a very holy day. On this day we recall that Christ, who was dead, rose again in the flesh.

Coupled with the miraculous circumstances of the birth of Christ, the events surrounding his death and resurrection were the most significant in the history of this world. Every one of us who has ever lived on earth is touched by what happened that first Easter nearly two thousand years ago. Surely this is a reason to celebrate Easter, so that we will remember what a difference it makes in each of our lives.

Easter is about hope.

If it weren't for the sacrifice of the Lord, if it weren't for that glorious Easter morning outside of Jerusalem, how would we feel facing death square on? How could we endure burying a loved one? How could we comfort an aged and ill parent or help a terminally ill friend or explain death to a stricken young person? How could we help the lost one? Fresh remembrance of what occurred *then* can enrich us, strengthen us, deepen our understanding about the purpose of life, and fill our hearts with hope—for we remember that we will not only live again after death, but we can live in peace, guilt-free, redeemed by our Lord Jesus Christ.

I am so deeply touched by these truths that I have chosen to share with you a few references from the Bible, to read from the actual account of the death and resurrection of Christ.

It is recorded in the gospel of John that on one occasion while Christ was instructing his disciples, he said to them: "I lay down my life, that I might take it up again. No man taketh it from me, but I lay it down of myself. I have power to lay it down, and I have power to take it again." (John 10:17-18.) Of course, the disciples didn't understand the meaning of this instruction. It was confusing, and they pondered his words. But from that point on in the ministry of Christ, the final, significant, and prophesied events took place in swift and tragic order:

The Last Supper, the ceremony of breaking bread and sipping wine in a sacrament of remembrance of the body and blood shed for us in Christ's sacrificial act.

The sop of friendship Christ gave to Judas, identifying his future betrayer.

Jesus Christ's washing of the feet of his disciples and his teaching that he who would be great must be a servant.

His taking time to teach them then of loving one another; and his giving them a new commandment to love others as they were loved by him.

Then, the walk to the Garden of Gethsemane, the prayer of agony, the sweating of blood, the betrayal, the capture, the mock trial—the crucifixion!

And after that earth-shaking event, the friends of Jesus Christ made arrangements to claim his body from the cross. This poignant moment in time has inspired countless masterpieces through the centuries, as artists have interpreted the hopeless, heartbroken, confused mood of those who had followed after Jesus Christ and now, seemingly, were left with only his pierced body to claim.

Joseph of Arimathaea, you remember, made arrangements for a new tomb in a little garden close by the hill of the skulls. The dead Christ was taken there, wrapped in new linens, and laid on a slab; then a huge stone was rolled into place to seal his safety.

Now, Mary Magdelene and the other Mary came

to the sepulchre early in the morning, on the first day of the week, to anoint Christ's body with precious oils. They were weeping, of course, for they loved him. But they found the tomb was empty, and they thought someone had taken the body away. The Bible tells us: "Now when Jesus was risen early the first day of the week, he appeared first to Mary Magdalene, out of whom he had cast seven devils. And she went and told them that had been with him, as they mourned and wept." (Mark 16:9-10.)

After that Christ appeared to two of his disciples as they walked a country road; and when they came to the little village, they begged him to stay with them. It is from the following passages in Luke that a favorite Christian hymn "Abide With Me" takes its text: "Abide with us: for it is toward evening, and the day is far spent. And he went in to tarry with them. And it came to pass, as he sat at meat with them, he took bread, and blessed it, and brake, and gave to them." (Luke 24:29-30.)

Christ had now made at least two appearances since his death on the cross. Each time, those who saw him were told by him to go and spread the word that he lived. Another appearance occurred when the eleven apostles of the Lord Jesus were gathered together in Jerusalem discussing the turn of events. Suddenly, though the door to the upper room was closed, the resurrected Christ himself stood in the midst of them and said unto them: "Peace be unto you. But they were terrified and affrighted, and supposed that they had seen a spirit. And he said unto them, Why are ye troubled? and why do thoughts arise in your hearts? Behold my hands and my feet, that it is I myself: handle me, and see; for a spirit hath not flesh and bones, as ye see me have. And when he had thus spoken, he shewed them his hands and his feet." (Luke 24:36-40.)

This account in Luke goes on to describe that Christ took the fish and honeycomb, and he *ate* with the apostles. Incredible! He ate with them. Afterwards he opened the eyes of their understanding "that they might understand the scriptures," which say: "Thus it is written, and thus it behoved

Christ to suffer, and to rise from the dead the third day: and that repentance and remission of sins should be preached in his name among all nations, beginning at Jerusalem. And ye are witnesses of these things. . . . And he lifted up his hands, and blessed them. And it came to pass, while he blessed them, he was parted from them, and carried up into heaven." (Luke 24:45-51.)

You know that you and I, too, through the power of the Lord, can be witnesses that these things are true. We, too, have been blessed by him. It seems to me that for our own sakes we should keep alive our testimony that Jesus Christ lives and cares about us. Then, to help others, we spread the good news that the risen Lord lives today and is our great and good friend, waiting to be gracious to us.

No wonder Easter is such a holy celebration.

Our hope this day is that for each of us Easter will be more than a time of new clothing and vacation from work and school, more than family gatherings, feasts, outings, and entertainment. Let us be thankful in remembering Christ again in faith, that our understanding may be opened by his spirit. You see, because of the meaning behind this day we can face death and not fear. We can find the courage to confess our sins. We have hope swelling our hearts that things finally will be all right.

I have been to Gethsemane. I have bowed my head at Golgotha. I have wept in the Garden Tomb near Jerusalem. I have studied the scriptural accounts and heard the testimonies of prophets. And I have my own witness as well—Christ lives!

I pray each of you may have the comfort of that witness this day and can join with me in saying, "I know that my Redeemer lives!"

The Life Twice Lived

The life recorded is the life twice lived.

Life, it is said, is God's gift to us, and what we do with it is our gift to God. I also hold to the idea that life is a grand adventure; whatever the particular details might be for us, our life is worth recording. Knowing this, we feel greater self-worth and are motivated to try a little harder to make each day a little better and ourselves a bit more noble.

We'll come to love our ancestors more too as we collect the happenings of their lives as well as the simple listings of names, dates, and places for our genealogical records.

It is my warm belief that living, recording, and remembering with a record is a delightful way to pass our season on earth. Experience has taught me that. I keep records. I search after the facts of life about loved ones. I know the joy that family and personal histories can bring. If I didn't know this, I wouldn't talk about it. It wouldn't seem right.

As we obediently write up a lesson learned, a hurdle leaped, we feel a surge of fresh appreciation to our Heavenly Father for his gift of life. It is good to be alive. It is satisfying to have lived a span. Even the most ordinary life seems extraordinary, the stuff movie scripts are made of, when its record at last reveals the copings and the yearnings, the setbacks and the small triumphs, the loving and the sacrificing.

Consider this portion of Milton L. Sharp's life story. I had a part in this incident, so it is especially interesting to me.

"I had a lead on a cemetery in the place my ancestors might have lived before moving west over a hundred years ago. Shelmadine is a family name. Shelmadine Springs is a tiny spot on the map of Pennsylvania. And I wanted to go there to see if that place had anything to do with my people.

"We hurried to find the cemetery in the Pennsylvania countryside before dark. We drove to the top of a lonely long slope, green-covered and tree-shaded, and came to a stop in the midst of the markers for the dead. There was mood here with a sky clearing from a twilight storm. The clouds, lightened now of their burden, clung to the hill beyond. The hill itself was layered with spring leafing and rich black-ribbon rows a cultivator had made. There were cow families in the valley between, each newborn wiggly-legged calf nuzzling its nonchalant mother. The secret to serenity lay in this scene.

"Our hearts soon caught the tempo, and we were close, at peace, for a time. Then the genealogy expert in the group detailed our errand, and we scattered among the sandstone shapes, eager to be first to find proof that my roots might have stemmed from here. Then we found it—a Shelmadine family marker. We circled it in excitement, jockeying for position, reading and talking and circling about the precious information carved into granite. Then we moved down the road to a private plot, abandoned now, where the sexton told us we might find further information.

"Beside a winding country road, with only a rickety, ragged pasture fence to secure the site, was a two-hundred-year-old burial place. The trees had grown huge around the old markers that had become enmeshed in the trunk forever. A single faint flag of the Revolution still flapped over a forgotten hero's grave. Smothered under layers of last fall's leaves were headstones tangled with blooming myrtle and lush ivy. It was a find we were unprepared for, and a paisley silk scarf was happily ruined in the scrubbing process to uncover data two hundred years old.

"There were cousins, a brother and sister, and two wives named Elizabeth on a single headstone, with the close dates of their untimely deaths summing heartbreak for a young husband. There were others. Did they watch nearby, hidden behind gnarled oaks? Did they wait anxiously to be discovered? Did they laugh at this frantic band of friends climbing over fallen markers and wild flowers to uncover yet another lost relative?

"No Shelmadines lived in Shelmadine Springs any longer, but there was evidence they'd been there once. A large family marker, an abandoned private cemetery, and a white-steepled country church with a brass marker mentioning it was bequeathed by Borndt Shelmadine to a Methodist congregation mark the sleepy village of Shelmadine Springs, Pennsylvania. Its founder lies buried on the green hill. But for me and mine he lives again in our hearts after our Shelmadine adventure."

A life recorded is a life twice lived. What a wonderful way to remember a precious hour of family discovery! A written record of a family with details of weather, setting, and mood that the mind might not furnish at a later time.

When we record our life or gather the details of an ancestor's, the next generation will know how we lived, what we learned, what we did, how we responded to what happened to us. The simple things we live by can prove powerful to others in their time of need. Someone has said that the present is understandable only in terms of the past. But with a life recorded, the future is wrapped in hope. No one ever really dies this way. A life is never finished when it can be picked up and lived again in the written world.

Eliza R. Snow was a pioneer poet who expressed the inner drive we all feel to be remembered.

> For friendship holds a sacred cord,
> That with the fibers of my heart
> Entwines so deep, so close, 'tis hard
> For death's dissecting hand to part.

I feel the low responses roll
Like far-off echoes of the night
And whisper softly through my soul,
I would not be forgotten quite.

And, my friends, neither would I and surely neither would you! Let's do better at recording this gift of our lives that God has given us. Remember, a life recorded is a life twice lived.

Of Wise Men and Shepherds

Charles Dickens wrote a special seasonal greeting to a family he loved. It said, "Merry, merry Christmases, friendships, great accumulation of cheerful recollections, affections on earth, and Heaven at last for all of us." I believe that about sums up the wonderful celebration we call Christmas.

Christmas is a beautiful time of the year. Hidden beneath the wrappings, among the greens and candle glow, behind the laughter and delightful confusion of gifts and gatherings, ever shines its secret—the ideal from our Savior's life and teachings that we love one another as he loves us.

Christmas is a time of awakening once more to that ideal. Have you noticed the special things that happen when families and friends and co-workers and sensitive strangers love each other in a Christlike way and then work at ever widening the circle of loved ones and dear acquaintances among the brotherhood of man? Have you noticed? I'm sure you have. You know, it is a kind of personal gift to me to be sharing Christmas thoughts with people who really understand what it is all about. In our separate ways or collectively as occasion calls, we can work at spreading the good news that Christ of whom we speak in our churches *was* that babe born in Bethlehem. He grew and waxed strong and became a necessary Redeemer for us all. He lives now and is keenly interested in us. He is the master implementer of God's plan of life for his children. He is the model of beautiful behavior one toward another. No wonder we love this time of the year when more of us pause to remember the ideal.

Christmas is about shepherds and wise men as

well as Christ. They worshipped at the manger long ago. We try to follow that pattern today.

Wise men are champions of Christ and his word, friends of the babe of Bethlehem and disciples of the Savior, interpreters of his word. There are wise women as well who arrange the festivities so that we are party to the right reasons and right feelings for the season.

And what of the shepherds who watch over the flock? Ah, to you who shepherd the work of the kingdom, we express our personal awareness of your worth. Whatever kind of place would planet earth be if there weren't some today who reached out to lift up the hands that hang down, to strengthen the feeble knees, to reassure the questioning heart? Whatever would we do if there weren't some among us who would keep the lonely vigil and go after the lost?

Living, working, serving, and suffering as Christ did before us rewards us with the inimitable warm, full feeling of Christmas. We know joy—the kind of joy only a closeness to the Lord can bring. He *is* there. He does live. He is waiting to be gracious to us. He was born to bear our burdens. But sometimes our faith falters, and we forget his love for us.

One evening I came home after a particularly tender and trying time with a relative of mine who lay suffering in the hospital. A woman I knew only slightly sat huddled by my door. She came to me because she needed someone outside herself. As I approached she scrambled to her feet and poured out her story of agony. I listened for a time and thought how different we felt in our problems. She was without hope. Then I stopped her in great concern and said, "My dear, don't you know that Christ lives?"

"Yes," she mocked, "I know that Christ lives. He just doesn't know that I live."

Then I had to turn into a good shepherd and lead her through basic truths until she knew peace and comfort again.

Maybe some of you have felt a loss of faith as you

struggle with your problems. I marvel at you who are striving to be supportive and pleasant with each other even under trying circumstances. My heart turns over as I sense your personal sacrifice to serve the widowed mother, the rebellious youth, the handicapped child, the heartbroken friend. Surely there are heavy hearts among us today. Some are going it alone. Some are sure they are failures. But I know that turning to Christ as a major part of the celebration this season will reawaken our knowledge that the Lord loves us and can lift us. We need not be without hope.

Consistently moving to me at this season is the story that centers in midwest America where a community was readying its annual nativity presentation. It seems to me I read it years ago in an old issue of *Guideposts*. It is now part of our family's Christmas lore.

The directors of this Christmas production had a problem. There was one little boy who was a bit slower than the rest—"not quite bright" was the phrase, I think, used in describing him. He had been a shepherd in the Christmas presentation for several years. You see, it was really the only part they could trust him with. But this was the last year he'd be eligible by age to participate in the holy pageant. What part could they give him for the last time? He surely couldn't be Joseph. To cast him as a wise man would be ridiculous. Finally, it was decided that he could handle the role of the innkeeper. All he had to do was shake his head and firmly declare that there was no room in the inn. So it was done, and they practiced and practiced with him so that all could go well on that all-important occasion.

The night of the performance the sacred story told in Luke unfolded before the community crowding the school auditorium for this traditional event. The young Mary and Joseph had reached the inn on the far side of the stage. The innkeeper answered their knock, and while prompters backstage and the audience en masse out front prayed silently, the slightly slow child came through. He responded according to cue, "No, there is no room in the inn."

Everyone breathed a sigh of relief.

Mary and Joseph turned and walked slowly away. But they acted so convincingly their parts of disappointment and worry that suddenly, much to everyone's dismay, the innkeeper ran after them calling, "Wait! Wait! You can have my room!"

There are those who thought the boy had ruined the play, that he had tampered irreverently with history. Others knew that the true spirit of Christmas had filled his heart.

Beginning with this season and carrying it forward, so must we be shepherds. As one of the lovely verses of Christmas suggests so well, "Let not our hearts be busy inns that have no room for Thee."

The stories, the verses, the singing, the symbols, and the legends are a precious part of the celebration. But may we remember that Christ and his ideals for us are no mere legend. He was that babe born in Bethlehem so long ago, born to redeem us. The wise men and the shepherds did follow that special star to Bethlehem. May we all be like them and come unto Christ anew at Christmas, loving him and each other more deeply, with more active concern. Then Christmas will be merry, hearts will be happy, and, as Dickens suggested, "heaven will happen at last for all of us."

Fly a Flag

Flags are attention getters. They stop traffic, start races, rally warriors, identify troops, promote patriotism, call a truce, and declare ideals. They also decorate, motivate, and educate.

Shakespearean enthusiasts knew the play was on when the white flag flew over old Globe Theatre. My neighbor with a pool raises a banner on her garden pole when she wants neighbors to know it's "open house" swimming—then the children come running.

The word *banner* comes from the Latin *bandum*, meaning standard.

The *American Heritage Dictionary* defines banner as a piece of cloth attached to a staff and used as a standard by a monarch, knight, or military commander; or an ensign bearing a motto or legend.

Banners, flags, ensigns, standards, and colors on staffs are historically exciting studies. They reveal the ideals of people, countries, armies, individuals, clans, and families. Heraldry designs were first used on the banners and shields of leaders of ethnically or politically united groups. It works just as well today.

One hears phrases such as, "the star-spangled banner," "holding aloft our colors," "posting of the colors," "raise an ensign unto the Lord," "present the standard," and "proclaim the standard" (as at ancient athletic games or modern youth rallies). A banner is evidence of what the bearer believes in, is committed to.

In ancient times a feudal lord or monarch used a piece of cloth attached to his staff as a rallying point. When the clans increased, confusion was avoided by emblazoning a distinctive, identifying symbol on the cloth. There was no question as to whose flag it was that way, and one didn't plunge headlong into the wrong rallying place.

If it worked for clansmen and warriors, why not for families, friendship circles, special interest groups? A friendly or family flag says not only who they are, but what they hold sacred, why they are banded together.

Our church was looking for a project to bring families closer together. A flag contest was suggested. The only rule was that the flag be three-by-five feet and that it identify the family some way in design—coat-of-arms, hobby, motto, family members, house, or activities.

One family made a flag showing hooped rings forming a circle with the motto, "We are together, now and forever," while another flag declared "Involvement is our motto." There are some subtle teachings going on each time the flag is flown in the presence of the children.

Another flag depicted the family hideaway, with members appliqued in colored scraps and stitchery standing cut-out-doll style beneath a pine. "United we stand" read that motto. Such a powerful rallying point! It's great when the whole family gets involved with the basic idea and the execution of the flag itself. Good family feeling is generated.

At the church function, incentive prizes were given for the most original, the finest workmanship, and the best idea. But everyone went home a winner with a personal flag to fly from the boat dock, the garden mast, the beach house patio, or beneath Old Glory on holidays at home.

A contest can be enjoyed among neighbors on a block, kids at school, members of a club, or people at the church. But who needs a contest when the new personal banner is a prize in itself?

There are many ways a banner or flag can be

used to make life richer, an occasion more memorable, or simply to proudly declare what is important to people.

In Salt Lake City during a Pioneer Days parade, fifteen hundred teenage girls marched as a unit, each carrying a banner she had made, declaring her heritage. The idea spread, and banner marches by young women are happening in Ohio, in New Jersey, in Oakland, in the Pasadena Rose Bowl, in Denver, and in Las Vegas. It could happen in your town, too.

Consider the delight a personal flag would bring as a gift to a beloved friend who has just been named Man of Distinction by his service club (or whatever). A bright, racing flag stitched up to float over water skiers makes an exciting hostess gift when you're invited for a weekend on the lake.

Weddings have taken on fresh moods. We know several families who liked the idea at our daughter's reception of flying a new flag especially created for the newlyweds. Some went ahead and fashioned their own banners to proclaim the beginning of a new household.

When a boy returns from the service or a girl is named Queen of the May, how about their own flag to mark the occasion? With today's homemaker eager for new arts-and-crafts projects, a personal, friendly, or family flag fills the need. And with an added bonus—an original banner rippling in the wind or decorating the mantel is enough to stir up ethnic pride in proud proportions.

You've heard of welcome mats being spread for special guests; well, in Scandinavia it's a welcome flag. When guests are coming, the national flag, the welcome flag, and often the guest's home country flag are flown above the door. I was charmed when I went to Oslo, Norway, to visit distant relatives there and found the American flag flying next to the Norwegian colors. I went home with a specially created welcome flag that had been raised with the other banners as a mark of honor to us as guests.

We admired a beautiful banner from a province in Italy. Sections of this banner had been hand embroidered by the young women in various towns and then put together to form a fine and elegant banner depicting their pride in their province and what it is famous for.

People care more about things that they have had a part in preparing or planning, don't they? It has been my experience that a deep commitment is felt by a person who thinks about what his or her standards are or what he or she holds sacred and who then goes to the trouble to sew, paint, weave, or silk-screen the motto on a banner. The same is true for family members or church groups. A flag or banner to rally around works miracles for *esprit de corps*.

Isaiah felt the benefit of banner imagery in teaching God's children. There are at least eight lifting references to banners or standards or ensigns in the book of Isaiah that are rousing to people who want to be identified as being on the Lord's side. I like this one especially: "Lift ye up a banner upon the high mountain, exalt the voice unto them, shake the hand, that they may go into the gates of the nobles." (Isaiah 13:2.)

Some time after the banner parade downtown, I watched a little boy laboring with crayons and colored paper for a long time. It was important work—I could tell that by the furrow in his brow and the pink tongue working around his lips. When the project was complete he shared it with me, and together we went out to his tricycle where he attached it to an old balloon stick held in place with masking tape. There was masking tape in many places besides where it was needed, and his effort wasn't a masterpiece by any stretch of the imagination. But when I saw a big smiling sun on his banner I felt good inside. "Well, your sun is just beautiful," I remarked to him.

"It's to remind me that Jesus wants me for a sunbeam," the little fellow explained seriously. And then he said, "Now I won't be afraid when I come to a steep hill going down."

The banners we make and the standards we fly can stir up important feelings in our own hearts for love of country, for love of God and his high principles for living, and for courage and love and many other important things we want to declare.

Say, let's go fly a flag!

Lessons in Family Letters

I don't know how you feel about reading somebody else's mail, but that's what we're going to do. These letters between family members have much to teach us. They are sort of love letters, and families are about love—or they ought to be.

Correspondence between family members is one of the most impressive ways of learning how people feel about each other. That's true if you are reading great-grandfather's love notes to great-grandmother, or if it's your own letter from a big sister who's married and has moved away. Letters are a great way of passing information from one generation to another, those things that need to be recorded. Advice can be given in letters to loved ones when they least suspect it and are most likely to listen.

There's another thing about family letters: they can be read and then put aside to be picked up again on a lonesome day to savor one more time. Letters can draw us close to each other when life is bent upon pulling us apart. There are eight of us in our family, and we're scattered from Lake Michigan to San Francisco Bay. Each month each one writes a family letter updating his or her activities. They are all sent to the current family historian who quick-copies them and sends a complete packet back to every other family member. It's wonderful. We've learned more about each other this way than we even knew when we were all home together. We've come to love and respect each other more as well as to help out in special ways. One letter called for the family to rally in fasting and prayer at a certain time for a member who was going through a particularly difficult time.

What a blessing this kind of tie is! You know, when these monthly packets come, it's like a warm reunion as we settle down to read the lot of them.

You and I are about to share adventures in people's lives through their letters. It really doesn't matter whose letters these are—at least not for our purposes now. They could be from your grandmother or mine. People aren't all that different. They do represent, however, a cross section of times, ages, and stages and experiences in life. Each lesson is important to us all. There is something we all can learn from these letters about family interaction and family feelings. We may even feel motivated to do some important corresponding of our own.

Just before the turn of the century a young Norwegian girl left everything and everyone she loved and emigrated to America alone. A pioneer town in Utah was a long way from Oslo, so she never returned to her native land. The letter writing was mostly one-sided because her parents weren't happy about her leaving. She wrote home regularly though, and those letters were faithfully and secretly saved by a devoted younger brother. When he died, the letters were passed on to his son, who carefully saved them in the attic for years.

Then one day the son of the emigrant girl, now himself an old man, went to Norway to visit the remaining relatives there. Life and heritage were precious to him as the tie in time became more evident. His past was now very vital to his future. What a thrill it was for him to be given the surprise packet of letters his mother had written over the years until shortly before her death! He'd been the youngest, and these letters were his only written record of her. As he read them, he loved her all over again and felt a sharp appreciation for her struggles and courage. They were simple letters and sparse; but what joy, as well as helpful facts about the family, they brought to the generation of her descendants!

Here are some excerpts: "Dear Unforgettable Mother: We are doing fine . . . usually we have enough to eat, but we have had quite a bit of illness lately . . . it is hard for us because we have no family close by to go to. I feel sorry for you and your illness, dear mother, and think about you often. I send you one dollar, and hope to send you more soon . . . I feel I should try and help you."

Later she learned that her mother had died, and she wrote, "Dear Brother Gustave: You were very young when I left, but now you are a grown man and I guess I would not recognize you. You wouldn't recognize me either. I am skinny and older and have lost quite a few teeth. P. S. Did mother speak of me before she died or ask you to send her regards?" Those questions tug at the heart. An old woman wanted the comfort of an aged mother she still loved. How precious and binding those family ties are! Why can't we see it sooner?

Here's a letter that is a bit of a commentary on a family's highly socialized life: "Dear Mom: Can we please stay home on Christmas day? I like to sit by the fire in the living room. I love you." That tells you something, doesn't it?

Letters can inform, motivate, remind, and comfort. As a parent communicates with a grown child away from home, she can pour out things she might be too self-conscious to say face to face. Listen to this letter:

"Dear Son: Grandfather is gone now, as you've heard. No more tricks or painfully familiar stories, but what I wouldn't give to hear one again. And no more sweet, affectionate hugs from this loving man as well as the stern reminders that Heavenly Father expects certain things of us.

"I wish I could truly tell you of the beauty I have felt, amid the trying times, in these last few days. My love for my father surfaced in a most satisfying way. I've felt deep love for him because of his giving me life and a certain quality of life; because he taught me to love sunsets and shooting stars, springtime and the brave crocus pushing up the last snow. I loved him because he fought to the finish, as he always has, trying to be spry and alert when he just didn't have it in him. People deserve to be around happy people was his philosophy. And I loved him then as he lay dying in the hospital, because he always gave love whether it was wanted or understood or even returned. So I thank Heavenly Father for a loving dad. I pray your goal will be to be such a one.

"People keep saying there are many kinds of love. I used to smile and nod in agreement. But now I know better. There really is only one kind of love, and that is the love that comes from our being Christlike. We show it in whatever appropriate way to child, friend, neighbor, or lover. Coupling and childbearing are an exquisite benefit of love; but if you don't nurture and protect and grow in Christ-likeness toward your partner, much is lost—maybe the whole marriage. I think the same is true for our family and friends and, ultimately, for all mankind. My father taught me by precept and example that God loves us all—each one the same. I realized that as I kissed your loving grandfather for the last time. And I love you, dear grown boy of mine. Take care. Mom."

There are lessons to learn from that letter, aren't there?

Adults look for opportunities to share their wisdom with children. It is best when it is done in tenderness and is written down so that the message can be referred to often.

The following excerpt is from a letter a grandmother wrote to her grandchildren. She is paralyzed from the waist down, and on one occasion she fell out of her wheelchair as she reached for something. She lay confined in a very narrow space, totally helpless and unable to save herself. She writes:

"The reason I've written this experience is to let you know just what took place and particularly what I was thinking about in that hour while I was lying so uncomfortably on the floor until help came. I didn't panic. In fact, my first thoughts were, *What a lesson this is!* A spirit of peace came over me as I asked myself the question, *How would you like to be sick in your spirit and too weak to rise? Imagine how terrified you would be if after death you were paralyzed in your spirit and had slipped and fallen from . . . the light of the Lord.* Instead of misery, I was filled with the spirit of prayer and gratitude. What a joy I felt to know that my physical handicap is so temporary! If I so comply, my spirit will soar high in the magnificence of freedom and light. As you grow in years and learning of life and the gospel, you will more fully understand this illustration your grandmother has written to you . . . meanwhile, children, learn what love means. Be kind—to one another and to everyone around. Kindness is the music of the world."

Louise Lake, who has friends all over the world because of her work with the National Polio Foundation, wrote that letter to her grandchildren. She is completely confined to her home now and enjoys every written encouragement.

I happened to be standing with a preschooler once in Piedmont, California, when the mailman made his delivery to the family home. The child took the mail and dropped it on a nearby table; as the letters scattered apart, a colorful commercially prepared envelope appeared. Walt Disney characters decorated it, and the little girl squealed with delight, "I have a letter. This one is for me!" Actually it was addressed "to occupant" and was advertising new home movie equipment, but I learned a lesson. I wish that I had written the letter she claimed. I wish that I had filled it with my love for her and my confidence in her and a sharing of some important, life-saving truths. Then when her mother read it to her, they'd both have been enriched.

Maybe we should get busy and write a letter to someone about how we feel, and what we are thankful for, what we remember about home, and how glad we are to be related to someone so special. If you have ever been alone for a time with life passing by full and demanding for everybody else and mainly meaningless for you, you know how a kind letter would lift.

Of course, we may not always get a letter when we need it, but we can write one so someone else will. Let's do it!

Linking

What Are You Going to Be?

Children have unusual ways of reminding us of some significant things, haven't they? They can even make grown men think, as I learned one day.

A little boy came clomping down the sidewalk in front of our house in his father's shoes; a tie was looped about his neck, and a man-size belt buckled tightly about his small waist dragged behind him like a tail. A kindly gentleman smiled at the child and asked, "Well, and what are you going to be when you grow up?"

"I'm going to be a daddy," said the boy quickly, flipping the tie. "See?" Then he looked up at the older man and asked the thought-provoking question, "What are you going to be when you grow up?"

The man was startled by such a precocious response, and it caused him to stretch his mind into eternity. After all, that was about the only place he had left to go. And in that context he had to admit to himself that, indeed, he still had some growing to do.

"I'm going to be a father," he solemnly said.

And commitment was born of that comment.

A man doesn't usually dream of becoming a heavenly school teacher or a heavenly engineer or a heavenly land-developer, let alone a heavenly father. Many hard-working men, if they think about life after death at all, have a comfortable view of a proverbial pink cloud and an eternity of lounging to the music of harpists—or something like that.

Our neighbor knew better than that. The boy's question reminded that grown man about eternity—about life forever, standing at the head of his own chain of descendants in the presence of God, our Father in Heaven.

Realizing that possibility would make a man think; and it suggests some growing up in a dramatic way, doesn't it? We will need to remember and practice the supreme example of the Savior who said, "What manner of men ought ye to be? Verily I say unto you, even as I am." (3 Nephi 27:27.)

Isn't it interesting that of all the titles of honor and admiration that could be given him, God himself chose to be called simply Father? Since we are in training in life to become like God, our neighbor's answer to the little boy's question was a good one. We are in eternity now, and we are rapidly becoming what we are going to be.

A friend of ours had struggled desperately for years with a drug habit. He had spent time in corrective institutions; his family's resources had been whittled by therapeutic, medical, psychiatric, and legal fees. But he made it. Then one day, when at last he was in the position of graduate student counselor to others who were now where he had been, he was asked by a teenage drug addict how he had won the battle.

"I'd never have made it if my father hadn't helped me," said the counselor.

"Your father helped you? How? My father is part of my problem," the teenager declared.

"Well, he prayed over me like an old-fashioned biblical patriarch," explained the counselor. "He prayed, and he listened to the Lord for guidance. He prayed about '*our* course of action' as if we were in it together. He prayed that neither of us would ever give up. He prayed over the professionals—that they would give me the right treatment. Then he would pray over me that I'd respond to their help, that I'd be able to resist temptation in the tough times, and that I'd be able to hang on and try and try again. And do you know, I well remember the day he laid his hands upon my head and called upon God to bless me and heal me. No, I just couldn't have made it without my father."

How fine a father, how superb a human being is the man who promises that his children in no way will be claimed by the adversary!

One such father spoke sternly to a threatened son, "Son, I'm giving you fair warning. I will never leave your side until you are back in our fold. I will personally pray for you and prepare and tutor you. I will comfort and counsel you. I'll try to be patient and forgiving. But together we'll both grow closer to what God wants each of us to be. Now forgive me, forgive me, my son, for past neglect and lack of understanding that might have brought us both to this tragic moment. What do you say we consider this our time of blessed awakening and get on with our task?"

The father kept his word. These two were subsequently seen everywhere together—on business trips, at the school games, at the gymnasium, at the library, on service projects, and in traditional church meetings. It worked.

Of course it worked. We may recall the thought from the Sermon on the Mount, "What man is there of you, whom if his son ask bread, will he give him a stone?" (Matthew 7:9.)

If we care about our children at all and if we stop to think about it, we'd not only give the child bread, we'd give him cake—we'd give him our full love, our full attention.

The question the little boy asked, "What are you going to be when you grow up?" becomes a spiritual guideline for those of us mature enough to be thinking beyond this life's professional pursuits.

What Is a Family?

Years ago Allen Beck started something when he wrote two charming pieces called "What is a Boy?" and "What is a Girl?" Today we'll take a look at what a family is—with apologies to Mr. Beck.

A family is God's way of blessing the world.

A family keeps a mother from doing the things she's always wanted to do until she is too old to do them. But somewhere along the way a family weaves such a magic that one day mother realizes that this, after all, *is* what she wanted to do all along. (As for fathers—they have to shave every day.)

Families are always multiplied by two and come in a wide range of mathematical combinations. This unique variety pack comes in assorted sizes, shapes, colors, dispositions, and bank accounts. Each additional member to the unit challenges, for a time, the lofty premise that all men are created equal—that newcomer gets more attention per hour than everyone else put together.

As we look at the individual components, it is easy to see what makes families exactly the way they are. From the youngest to the eldest, each member has a part to play.

The youngest member of the circle is termed the baby. This has nothing to do with age, actually, but rather a stage of being; for whether six months or sixty years old, the youngest child is persistently referred to as "the baby."

Babies are for picking—picking at, picking up, and picking up after. Babies are also for kissing and caring and diapering and for bedding and bottling, for holding and hugging.

They come equipped with an amazing gift for melting the most rugged father into a reasonable facsimile of jelly and convincing a mother that she'd rather have her hands in detergent than suntan oil any day.

Babies cause parents to love each other more deeply, to smile more through tears, to buy more film, lose more sleep, stay home from more parties, and become more painful bores. But they also remind them that heaven is really very close after all.

Yes, babies are for loving.

The next age group in the family is the toddlers. These little destroying angels may be found wherever there is water. They are also known to slide down the best furniture, sneeze when fed, and move restlessly from room to room leaving their trail behind them. The only time they are quiet is when they are doing something they shouldn't. Toddlers have a disarming way of charming. They smile their sweetest smile when they are about to be disciplined.

Toddlers are on the threshold of a great new world of learning. So toddlers are for teaching—teaching to sing, to pray, to read, to eat with forks instead of fingers, to understand that training pants are the road to freedom, to know right from wrong, and to recognize the difference between Jesus and Santa Claus. One of the nicest things about a toddler is that he loves you unabashedly, anyway.

Oh, toddlers are for loving.

Then there is that delightful stage when offspring can now advance to the nearest grade school. Grade schoolers are famous for giggles and gum, for the blank spaces in the front of their smiles, for freckles sprinkled generously across the bridge of the nose, and for telling family secrets to neighbors.

They have a talent for running—running noses, running away and running errands, and for running the bathroom water the longest with the least to show for it. They are for getting—measles at Christmas, and into trouble when you aren't looking. They are skilled at getting things into drawers already too full, and other things out of closets that shouldn't have been opened in the first place. They ask more questions and eat more times a day than you had in mind. They are just great at losing boots, sweaters, one glove, balls, books, lunch pails, and instructions. They are devoted to creatures of the earth that growl, slither, wiggle, or crawl. Grade schoolers have been known to collect bottles, rocks, wrappers, and a fan club made up of proud parents and grandparents, of teachers and big sisters, especially when they perform in the school program.

Oh, grade schoolers are for loving.

Teenagers in the family grow too much too soon, or too little too late. They make us proud with their beauty of body, quickness of wit, fierce loyalties, and the fact that they remembered our birthday with an extravagant gift without being told.

They are the challenge and the challenger. They challenge our authority, our decisions, our life-style, our system, our taste in music, and our turn to have the car.

They emerge smarter, stronger, and more spiritual than we. But let us remember that we lifted—dragged, fought, loved?—them to where they are today. We just won't talk about it in front of them—it would ruin the whole thing.

Yes, families are God's way of blessing the world, of shaping a strong, stubborn man into a strong, sensitive father, and a beautiful, bossy woman into a beautiful, blessed mother.

Families are for loving each other anyway. Yes, a family is God's way of blessing the world. Oh, thank God, families are forever!

A Spark of Divine in Us

I rode in a bus in Osaka with a group of Americans and Japanese—some older, some younger, but brothers and sisters all in their hearts. The American visitors sang one verse of "I Am a Child of God" in English. The Orientals sang the next verse in their native tongue. It was a warm and wonderful exchange of brotherly love.

Mormon children started singing this song years ago, but now I hear people across the world enjoying its uplifting words and pleasant time for community singing.

Our feeling of self-worth grows and swells significantly when at last we come to believe that we are, in fact, children of God. There is a spark of the divine in us. We have spiritual roots. "The Spirit itself beareth witness with our spirit, that we are the children of God." (Romans 8:16.)

It was the young father's first child. His wife's parents were serving a mission abroad, and so his own mother had accompanied them to the hospital for this momentous occasion. The young father went into the delivery room to watch the miracle of birth. The grandparents waited just outside the door. At the first sound of the baby's cry, the door flew open and the excited young man rushed out to announce the news.

"It's a boy! A boy! And I just love him!"

He had hardly had time to check over his new baby, much less build up any kind of relationship with him, but he loved him already. The baby was something he had helped to create. Therefore, he was worth loving.

The grandmother looked at her son, the new father, and smiled knowingly. "Isn't it wonderful? Do you know that is exactly the way I feel about you?"

"It is?" The son was surprised. His mother loved him the way he loved that new boy child in there? How could that be? He looked at her, somewhat embarrassed. He didn't feel the same way about her as he did about that remarkable little bundle.

"Yes," she said. "You are my firstborn. I love you freely, as you love your own baby. But just remember, he probably won't feel much different toward you than you do toward me. My reward is that you love your children as I love you. Though it may be hard to believe at this moment, your heart will expand in parenthood and you'll love all your children as much as this one. There's another perspective to this situation, too. Our capacity to love our children cannot begin to compare with Heavenly Father's. You now have a little idea of how much Heavenly Father loves you. One day you'll learn to love Heavenly Father as your boy will learn to love you."

Important lessons in love were learned that morning in a hospital corridor. A parent goes on loving a child whether love is returned or not. The heart expands with boundless love, and each additional child is welcomed the same as the first. Unselfish love is Christlike love. It knows no bounds. It seem incredible until the experiences of life and love thrust it upon us. Then it is like a great door of understanding opening for us. In such a setting, we can begin to appreciate the scripture, "Remember the worth of souls is great in the sight of God." (D&C 18:10.)

Someone has defined love as ultimate concern. Surely our Heavenly Father cares in the extreme what happens to us, just as we care about our own offspring. The Savior's primary concern on earth, the full sweep of his mission, proved the worth of souls before God. He came that men might have life, and have it more abundantly. He taught the value of the individual over tradition, customs, rules, and laws in a day when the Pharisees were concerned over the letter of the law.

Christ taught that there is no rest from the work of saving souls. He taught that the publican, the sinner, and the saint alike are counted precious before God and that the gospel is for the sacred purpose of molding the soul to make it ready for celestial life and all the joyous blessings God has in store for us.

Christ taught the great concern of God for all men, including the lost and the low. He used three powerful parables to give us insight into how precious everyone is to him. In the parable of the lost sheep, the shepherd left the flock to find the sheep that had strayed. He brought it back to the fold and cried, "Rejoice with me; for I have found my sheep which was lost." (Luke 15:6.) In the parable of the lost coin, a search located that money which was lost, and again we read, "Rejoice with me; for I have found the piece which I had lost." (Luke 15:9.) In the parable of the lost son, the prodigal's wayward ways lost for him all that was valuable in life. He finally turned homeward, repentant; and his father, seeing him far off, "ran, and fell on his neck, and kissed him." (Luke 15:20.)

In each case the Savior compared that which was lost to the soul of man and pointedly declared that there would likewise be much joy among the angels over one sinner who repents.

We cannot study the parables or the life of the Savior and his ministry without being warmed to our personal value to our Heavenly Father, his Son Jesus Christ, and the heavenly hosts. In fact, the scriptures remind us that God so loved us that he sent his only begotten Son to atone for our sins, to suffer, to be crucified, and to die for us. (See John 3:16.) Salvation now is ours.

So, we are children of God. Each of us is endowed with certain unique personal gifts, is a recipient of special gospel blessings, and is a member of a covenant people with a vitally important job to do.

With all of this going for us, we should marvel at our station in life. Lethargy and despondency should have no place in us. Instead, we should be motivated to reap the fullness of our privileged condition by continuing to repent, change, and beautify our lives.

Consider this quotation from C. S. Lewis in his book *Mere Christianity*: "Imagine yourself as a living house. God comes in to rebuild that house. At first, perhaps, you can understand what He is doing. He is getting the drains right and stopping the leaks in the roof and so on: you knew that those jobs needed doing and so you are not surprised. But presently he starts knocking the house about in a way that hurts abominably and does not seem to make sense. What on earth is He up to? The explanation is that He is building quite a different house from the one you thought of—throwing out a new wing here, putting on an extra floor there, running up towers, making courtyards. You thought you were going to be made into a decent little cottage: but He is building a palace."

What a blessing to be so loved by a Heavenly Father! If he as well as our earthly parents care so much about what happens to us, surely we should care enough about ourselves to continue to grow and change and appreciate the spark of the divine in us.

An Eggbeater in the Silver Chest?

*B*rides magazine conducted a poll, and this response is heartwarming in today's environment of live-in love arrangements: getting married is coming back in style. Ninety-nine percent of those polled reported that a legal ceremony accompanied by all the traditional trappings was most desirable.

But after you are married, then what?

December is rivaling June as the big month for weddings, from all reports. Yet it seems fitting—giving each other the gift of self is highly appropriate in a season of high celebration about ultimate giving.

To the brides and the grooms we say, since you've fallen in love some changes have come. You two who were friends now look at each other and the world around you with an eye single to your own needs. Out of all the faces in all the world, this one face is your kind of face; this one smile, the warming one.

You build your dreams, set the date, and go through the motions of betrothal. And while that enchanting spell spreads over you, the wedding date finally comes; and you two, holding hands, walk off into the sunset to live happily ever after.

New in your discovery of each other's delightful qualities is the discovery of each other's ways in the daily tasks of life. You are full of wonder, all right; but you wonder, too, how you could not have suspected that this marvelous skier would decorate the bedroom with socks, boots, and used lift passes.

And when he dries the dishes, he absentmindedly puts the egg-beater in the silver chest.

He, meanwhile, wonders how you, his beautiful and adorable wife, could possibly emerge as a toothpaste-tube mutilator, a cap leaver-offer, a financial hazard with a checkbook. What's more, you washed his whites with a red sock entangled.

Now the wonder may turn to wondering whether two people so different, though once cloaked in love, can ever become one.

It is at such moments of wonder that you can feel glad that you are friends as well as husband and wife. You can be thankful for happy memories and precious investments of time together. You're grateful for an understanding of God's plan of life and the potentiality of the human spirit. In all of your differences there is one important quality you two share—imperfection and the right to personal improvement. And you've made a commitment.

So, in sweet patience—a patience that grows in the practice of it—you try again: she picks up the socks; he replaces the toothpaste cap; she retrieves the eggbeater; he copes with the overdraft one more time. Then you kiss each other in a new kind of loving. The happily-ever-after idea becomes a stronger possibility instead of a romantic myth.

There is a classic bit of Christmas literature, "The Gift of the Magi," by O. Henry, that ideally describes giving to each other. It is the story of the poverty-stricken lovers who had no gifts to give at the Christmas season. Finally the wife, whose beautiful long hair was indeed her crowning glory, had her hair cut to sell; and she used the money to buy a platinum chain for her husband's prized possession, his gold watch. He, in similar unselfishness, sold his treasured timepiece to buy a pair of tortoise-shell combs for his wife's cascade of brown hair. It is a tender story. Their unselfish gifts made them grow in love.

Perhaps you two aren't the perfect partners yet. But you're in good company, and you keep on trying because you promised you would. You are two imperfect children of God who now look at each other and the world around you with an eye single to another's needs.

You are friends and lovers still. What, after all, does an eggbeater in the silver chest have to do with anything?

Mother's Day

Mother's Day reminds me of a television program in which a young kindergarten teacher grandly remarked: "I start four- and five-year-olds on the path of scholarship, leadership, and a lifetime of integrity. I also pour juice."

Well, to all you mothers and surrogate mothers—to all you juice pourers within the sound of my voice, we give you honor and greeting.

If you are new at the business of mothering, enjoy it while your baby simply cuddles and coos.

If you are older and weary of the work, take heart that you are thought about on countless occasions that have nothing to do with the holiday set aside to insist upon remembrance through gifts and prescribed tenderness. Who among you, mothers, does not recall with a special clarity and with a tender tug of the heart her own mother? Of course! Then take comfort that along with happy wishes and congratulations of the day, we pause to remind you that you are not forgotten. When you have mothered, you have left an indelible mark. Your wisdom, your endless outpourings of food, clothing, bandages, juice, and comfort are recalled by your children as love upon request, love unconditional, love when no one else shows it, love when it is deserved least. Oh, you are remembered. You are appreciated. You are loved. Such feelings surface in unusual settings, but they are there and are payment aplenty for your caring.

A funeral service was under way for the mother of five young children. She had taken her own life in a way that broke the hearts of her family and set the neighbors to gossiping. Somehow the speakers and the musicians had mocked their way through appropriate thoughts and melodies. The religious leader had preached his sermon. Suddenly a child about ten left her place beside her grieving father and walked up to the pulpit unannounced, unscheduled, and unabashed. Maybe she'd heard the whispers of neighbors. Maybe she had some doubts of her own. Surely she'd had her struggles in a home where trauma was deep enough to bring such a tragic end to a life. Yet this little girl taught the lesson of the day when she said: "I loved my mother. Please talk nice about her. She was good to me, and she smelled so good every morning."

We went home humbled, and diligently resolved to smell good every morning. It was the least we women could do, and it might make all the difference.

A great civic and church leader whose influence has been felt worldwide credits his widowed mother for shaping his beginnings and for being a lifelong influence. In *Gifts from a Mother* Elder Marion D. Hanks writes:

"One night while I was still attending school and living at home with Mother, I returned just past midnight to find the light in Mother's little front bedroom still burning. I went to her and sat on the bed and jokingly chastised her a little for staying up so late. 'What are you doing with your light still on at this hour?' I asked her.

" 'I'm waiting for you,' she said.

" 'Oh,' I said, 'and did you wait up for me every night while I was on a mission and away at school and in the South Pacific in the war?'

" 'No,' she said, 'that wouldn't have been possible. No, I just got on my knees here by this bed and told the Lord about you, told Him how I felt about you and the kind of man you are and my dreams and aspirations for you. I asked Him to preserve you from evil, and to help you do your duty for your country courageously. Then I climbed into bed and left you in His hands and went to sleep.'

"I kissed her and bade her goodnight and went to my own quiet place and to my knees and gave thanks to God for such a mother." Then he went on to quote Coleridge: "A mother is a mother still, the holiest thing alive."

A friend of mine had enjoyed a rich and lengthy life with a husband who loved her and whom she adored. They'd struggled trying to build a family. Together they'd buried precious loved ones, adopted a child to fill empty heart places. They had coped with financial disaster, awesome professional responsibility, some grave disappointments, and finally with sweet public success.

Out of the details of their life, such closeness came that when death claimed the husband, the woman felt the sun would never shine again. She wondered that people walked the city streets smiling. Then one day she responded to a need and took a volunteer assignment in a local pediatrics hospital. Her job was to register the children being brought there for medical help. All day long she dealt with people with problems, but she was oblivious to them because she wallowed in her own grief. One day there came a mother with a baby so deformed and pitifully stricken that my friend was startled out of her self-centered blindness. The mother of the stricken child was cheerful and friendly and reached into the heart of this widow in a way that swept away bitterness. The baby's mother was a "blessings-counter" and told the widow that she felt especially honored to be given this particularly troubled baby, this unfortunate bit of humanity to care for. "God gave this baby to me because he knew I'd love him well. Isn't that an honor for me?"

A mother taught another mother the lesson of gratitude and confidence before God.

So, mothers, we give, we teach, we lift, we comfort, we pray, and we pour a lot of juice; and somewhere along the way we experience the truth recorded in Proverbs: "Her children arise up, and call her blessed." (Proverbs 31:28.)

But even if they don't, those of us who have mothered know that, like virtue, mothering is its own reward.

Father's Day

One of the most impressive reports about fathers to be made public was an article describing an effort undertaken in an Indianapolis school district to get fathers interested in their children's school life. It seems the fathers hadn't been supporting the PTA. But there was one teacher in a certain school district who counted a father's influence as so vital to the success of the school child that she determined to find a way to lure fathers into the classroom. Once there, she was sure she could excite them about what their children were doing and convince them of needing their help for greater achievement on the part of their offspring.

She assigned her class members to write an essay, "What I Like About Daddy," and urged them to be specific. A note was sent home announcing the date when these essays would be read out loud in a PTA meeting. It was a meeting the fathers supported.

They came in their small cars, their campers, their super specials. They came in suits and ties, blazers and golf shirts, pullover sweaters and plaid shirts with button-down collars. Some came right off the job in their jump suits and parkas, slicked up some for the school meeting. They all came reflecting their daily work, their life-style, and their personal taste.

They came because they were curious and somewhat apprehensive, too. What would these little children have to say about their fathers?

Now some interesting things happened when the papers were read. First a random selection had been made from a box full of essays. Letter after letter proved to be quite similar. Each child, according to the assignment, listed what he or she liked about daddy. Some said he'd built a doll house, or helped fatten a pig to sell, or taken them on a trip, or played catch on the lawn out back. But out of 326 letters the overall thrust was that kids liked their dads because they spent time with them. In all those letters they credited dad with helping or giving something they needed as being a reason for liking him. Not one out of the 326 mentioned what kind of car he drove, how he dressed, where he earned his money, or what size house he'd provided for them. They didn't even describe the way he looked—bald, bearded, tall, or overweight. It was just that dad was great because he was a friend in some way to his child.

Now, every man came to that meeting with his own opinion of himself and an image of his contribution to his child's life. No doubt there was some guilt felt as he anticipated his shortcomings and which of them the child would describe before the class. Each went away knowing for certain that he was important to his child in terms of the time he spent doing things with that child. It could be chores or flying kites—but it was time in the company of that father that got written about.

During war years the stories of heroism of soldiers and loyalty to country fill the press. But one of the most touching to me is the story about a lonely spot during the Vietnam crisis when a young chaplain was conducting a worship service for the soldiers. The mix at the meeting was across the rank—all levels of enlisted men and commissioned officers sat together seeking strength, worshiping God, their Heavenly Father. Suddenly, as the meeting progressed, it was noted that a broad smile lighted the face of the chaplain. Soon the men saw the reason for that smile. A special guest had come in and walked toward the stand to sit in a chair reserved for him. The plane bringing dignitaries had been delayed, so the meeting had started without them. The interruption was not a surprise; a guest had been expected. Only it was a surprise that the chaplain's father was a last-minute substitute guest for one who had been unable to keep the assignment. Father and son smiled at each other, shook hands, and then embraced each other for long minutes. Many respectful, homesick men wept as they watched. It was as if every son were in the arms of his own father again, such was the vicarious joy of that scene. Some had never had the blessing of such a relationship bond with their own fathers that would equal the love and companionship exhibited in that tender scene of reunion.

It isn't so much what you had from your father as what kind of father you are that counts. One has some control over that.

Wanting to be a good father and being one aren't exactly the same, but good intentions are helpful. One young man told us of his wonder at becoming a father. He said he fell in love with a beautiful campus queen and married her in fine style. Later, he said, he turned into a father when his wife brought forth their firstborn son. The new father said he felt totally unprepared for the experience of fatherhood, and he winced at the incredible responsibility of it as he beheld the miracle of his offspring. "But I loved him. I do love him," he emphasized brightly, "and I'll love him enough to make up for my unpreparedness. How does a boy prepare to be a father, anyway?"

How, indeed? we might echo. Yet implicit in that sharing is the secret, it seems to me. He loved that baby. If he goes on loving him into manhood, someday a reunion like that one described in Vietnam may take place after years of separation because of school, service for one's country, employment, marriage—or death. Love is the element; and showing it through time spent together was what the children in the Indianapolis school bragged about.

One of the favorite pictures in our family album is

the one taken when our son was three years old, wearing his red and blue sweater, sitting with legs swinging free on a chair beside his father's bed, singing him a nursery song to make him better after a serious accident. That picture reminds the whole family now of the hours of devoted care the child showered upon his tall dad during the weeks of recuperation. He did not weary, that little one, of his well-doing. He sang his songs over and over again faithfully. He drew pictures on dad's arm and softly stroked his hair. Books and friends were left aside because his father seemed to need him. Indeed, father purred under such attention. That kind of tender, loving care doesn't happen with sunshine and rain. It comes because a father has loved a little boy enough to win undying affection. A relationship like that has its own reward during later and more trying years.

I think of a young friend of mine whose father was a wheelchair arthritic for all the time my friend grew from a child into a teenager. Neighbors first were worried and then became pleasantly accustomed to the exciting ride to church the boy gave his dad in the wheelchair each week. The son was sure-footed and firm gripped. He'd send his father scooting and then run and catch him as they both laughed out loud. Dad had been a ski patrol hero before illness struck. It was a time of special sharing for these two that sweetened the life of both. They loved each other, we all knew, and that's what counted.

One Father's Day program featured family speakers to pay tribute to their fathers. One of the trembling teenagers, with his voice changing and his hands shaking on the papers he held, let the tears flow freely when he looked down at his dad sitting there before him and said: "My father is just like I want him to be. He comes home from work and kisses Mama and lifts the baby up and makes her laugh. He runs his fingers through my little brother's hair and says, 'How's my little man tonight?' Then he puts an arm around me saying, 'I am proud of my big boy. Did things go all right today?' "

The boy stopped after reciting several special

incidents that proved his father was a good man. His voice faltered, and he wiped a tear as he finished, "I love my dad. I wish I'd heard him tell me he loved me."

There are many ways to show love, but sometimes we need to say the words. That young man's talk reminded us of that. Let us each express to each other, fathers to sons and back again, parents to children, wives to husbands, "I love you." Which translated means, "You're special to me. You make my heart warm. I'm glad we are related."

What's in a Name?

A person's name is his most precious possession next to life itself. It is his identity. It sets him apart from others. I remember the story of the freshman at a great university who was homesick and disgruntled because nobody knew him and he knew nobody else. The thousands of people who tramped across campus were strangers to each other and known to the administration by the number on their computer registration card. He wrote home the sad lament that it wasn't until he bent his computer card that he was plucked out of the crowd and noticed. Oh, what's in a name!

As I travel throughout the world I find myself increasingly fascinated by people's names and the story behind their naming.

Upon returning from an assignment in Europe, I gained a perspective that has set me thinking about names. There I met delightful women and girls named Birgitta, Marja, Kristin, Kari, Hilma, Anja—and a whole new batch of little ones named Camilla! It seems that the visit made there by President Spencer W. Kimball and his wife, Camilla, is remembered with warmth and purpose.

There are many little boys named Spencer these days too, all over the world, wherever the Kimballs have traveled.

A time ago we had a party at our home for a special family occasion. We were honored that President Kimball and his wife, Camilla, came. As I was welcoming them, my sister quickly brought her little son over to meet them.

"President Kimball," she said, "this is Mark Spencer Cook. He was named Spencer after you."

President Kimball bent his knees so that he could look eye-to-eye with this little boy. Then he took the child's hand firmly in his own and said, "Well, do you know what I give to little boys named Spencer?"

"No." A shy reply.

"I give them a dollar. Camilla, do you have a dollar?" Obviously Camilla Kimball is very important to her husband. When she took upon herself his name, as Mrs. Spencer Woolley Kimball, she accepted all the wonderful delights as well as the vital little duties that a wife is entitled to.

People in all cultures have named their children after heroes or heroines, after distinguished ancestors, after presidents and dictators. If a child is well named, it is assumed he will emulate his namesake. But it is no mere gentle gesture to move from having someone's name to being like him or her. They have to live as their namesake lived and keep the same standards.

So, though a little girl may be named Camilla and a boy be called Spencer, this does not guarantee they will be like them—president or partner to a president, as the case may be. There is, of course, much that can be said for the power of suggestion.

For those of us who have formally taken upon us the name of Jesus Christ, what does this mean to us, specifically? What difference does this make in our lives? How does this set us apart from others in the world—this taking upon us the name of Jesus Christ?

We meet in the name of the Lord. We pray in his name. We covenant in his name. We take his name upon us in sacred ordinances, and we witness that we are willing to take upon us the name of Jesus Christ that we may always remember him, that we may become like him, and have his spirit to be with us. Whatever the nagging or sweet details of life, this is vitally important—to have his spirit to be with us. Now, if we take upon us the name of ·Jesus Christ, we take upon us the obliga- tion and beautiful blessing of being obedient to his will for us.

As we take upon us his name, we share in it. In return, he endows us with the gifts of the Holy Ghost—with power to testify of him to others, power to be effective in our service, power to discern needs, power to determine truth. And we receive promptings necessary for making sound value judg- ments. When we covenant with the Lord to take upon us his name, we also take upon us the burden of helping mankind in a special way.

So whether we are named Spencer, Adam, Ronald, Winston, Ruth, Birgitta, or Camilla, if we take upon us the name of Jesus Christ we take upon ourselves his ways, his will, and his work, as well as his name.

An ancient ruler named King Benjamin gave a powerful counsel to his people shortly before he died. He taught of Christ, pointing up His sweet example of obedience to God, of kindness and forgiveness, of patience and integrity, of powerful and unconditional love. He explained the details of what people should do if they were to be like Christ. The people were deeply touched at the conclusion of this inspired sermon and cried out in one voice that they wanted to make a covenant to be like the Savior.

Then King Benjamin said to the people: "Ye have spoken the words that I desired; and the covenant which ye have made is a righteous covenant. . . . There is no other name whereby ye can be made free. There is no other name given whereby salvation cometh; therefore, I would that ye should take upon you the name of Christ." (Mosiah 5:6, 8.)

King Benjamin went on to encourage their obedience to the teachings and example of Christ, promising them eternal life if they would but do so. We all should live as disciples, shouldn't we? Shouldn't we behave as if we had taken upon ourselves the name of Christ?

If we will begin to do this, we will soon notice an important dimension. Trials and troubles won't get the better of us. Our hearts and our homes will be filled with unspeakable love. Our units of worship will be stronger and our numbers will swell. Good will be done. You see, taking upon us the name of Christ and living as if we have *can* make all the difference.

One final thought. As we said a moment ago, a person's name is precious to him! Surely we should not take anyone's name in vain, bringing it dishonor or judging unfairly. This is true of God, too. He has commanded us to hold his name sacred, as it is recorded in Exodus 20:7: "Thou shalt not take the name of the Lord thy God in vain; for the Lord will not hold him guiltless that taketh his name in vain."

What's in a name? Everything that person stands for. It's true of you, it's true of Christ, and it's true of God the Father.

Woman's Precious Energies

One of our four daughters was born trailing clouds of womanly glory. Her girl-skills were absolutely innate, natural, winning. Even as a tiny child she knew how to influence men and make them feel marvelous. Whenever a man of any age came to visit in our home, she would quickly toddle off to find some little treasure and lay it at his feet. Startled though they might be by such unbidden attention, young and old alike were all smiles—charmed at being chosen, warmed by such caring. She grew up looking for opportunities to temper rough lives by lovingly encouraging, quietly caring, and tirelessly using her gifts and skills to bless those around her. She's a young mother now and tends children of working women so that the little ones can have gospel training they might not get at a day-care center, or she takes a troubled teenager into their little family circle for a time of healing, and she still makes her husband feel he's the happiest man on earth. She is forever laying a little treasure at his feet, so to speak.

The motive and focus of her efforts are unselfish. She was born with womanly traits, it's true, but more important she has cultivated them over the years. And that has made all the difference to her as well as to everybody else who comes within her circle of influence.

I have come to believe that there is nothing enduring in life for a woman unless it is what she instills in the lives of her friends and in the hearts of her loved ones and from there to others who come within her sphere. This is the best way a woman can serve her Heavenly Father. To be an extension of his spirit in the lives of his children is the only cause grand enough for woman's precious energy. It's her only real fulfillment.

Women probably aren't to be without a certain restlessness in all of today's commotion about their role. Social change is ever with us. Any new idea or attitude thrust upon us by the world, however, should be carefully weighed against the eternal scheme of things. Actually, today's women have more "rights" and more status than they have ever had before, and yet a large segment of today's women don't seem to be any happier because of it. Surely they're not safer on the streets!

It seems obvious that women need more encouragement to understand their roles as influencers. We all hope a generation will be raised up who will be law-abiding instead of dishonest; unselfish instead of dollar-matching; helpful instead of indifferent; courageous instead of self-conscious. We need women to influence, teach, and nurture; to love and pray little people and bigger ones into moral, caring people.

Margaret Mead, a famous sociologist, pointed out that through the ages human beings have remained human largely because there were women to provide continuity to life—to be there when loved ones go to sleep and when they wake up; to listen to tales of broken hearts; to soothe, support, sustain, and stimulate husbands and sons as they face the vicissitudes of the hard outside world; and to be models for girls in a new and needful world.

I believe that's really it—women provide continuity of purpose and being, in an often frightening world where changes in values and behavior can be far more disturbing than those developments in technology or in an arms race. A woman is God's special helper in giving life, but also in shaping the course of life.

Tabitha, or Dorcas, as she was called, was a very special woman who lived in Joppa in the time of Peter. The Bible tells us that Dorcas was full of good works and almsdeeds which she did. Then suddenly she became ill and died, and life changed for all in her circle. Neighbors and friends were distraught with grief and sent for Peter to hurry to the bedside. There are touching details of how the people begged Peter to heal Dorcas. They showed him the clothing she'd made for them. The widows she had helped wept.

And then in Acts we read: "Peter put them all forth, and kneeled down, and prayed; and turning him to the body said, Tabitha arise. And she opened her eyes: and when she saw Peter, she sat up. And he gave her his hand, and lifted her up, and when he had called the saints and widows, presented her alive. And it was known throughout all Joppa; and many believed in the Lord." (Acts 10:40-42.)

There are several important things to remember from this story. First, Tabitha helped those in need. Second, those who had been helped were grateful for everything she had done. Third, in faith they called upon the priesthood, who prayed before turning to the stricken woman. Fourth, the healing took place through a servant of the Lord. And fifth, credit was given the Lord, for it was his power working through a servant on earth that raised Tabitha from the dead. Sixth, many believed on the Lord because of these happenings.

All this because of one woman's good works.

In 2 Kings is the report of the little captive maid who dared to suggest to her new master, Naaman, proud captain of the enemy hosts, that if he would visit her Israelite prophet, Naaman would be healed from his leprosy. This he did. The lesson about false pride is often preached, but we don't often hear about the "little captive maid" who made all the difference.

If a young captive maid can have such an influence, so can all young girls in all their circles. The world could be turned around. Influence of a good woman can stem the tide of error and produce a more noble generation.

A great modern prophet, Spencer W. Kimball,

has said: "I hope our young women will establish early in their lives a habit of Christian service. When we help other people with their problems, it puts ours in fresh perspective."

I heartily agree with that counsel. To be an extension of Christ in the lives of his children is the only cause grand enough for woman's precious energy.

A Lot of Good People Out There

Frequently we are reminded of unpleasant things that people are doing in the world. The media spreads the stories daily. But we know there are a lot of good people out there who are making a good difference to the quality of life.

There are a lot of good people out there who are doing common things in an uncommon way and making this world a nicer place to be. Ann Morrow Lindbergh wrote, "My life cannot implement in action the demands of all the people to whom my heart responds." We understand that dilemma, yet it is heartening to see many people quietly doing good in spite of their own pressures. Here's one example:

A family had put everything on the line to help their father during a bitter political campaign. He lost. Six children close together in age had worked long and hard. They were new to this kind of disappointment and took the defeat painfully. With defeat went hope of financial recovery as well, because few people want to pay the political debts of the loser.

The day after the voting, the family gathered glumly about the table, trying to bolster each other's spirits during dinner. A neighbor knocked at the door and followed the mother back to the dining room. Rather than accept their invitation to sit with them, he stood at one end of the room and began talking to them. He wasn't someone they'd been particularly close to. His business was in Detroit, and he seldom was home; but he knew something about heartbreak and dashed dreams. He told the family about the need for people to help make our communities better places for families to live. He praised the father as one who was willing to get into the thick of things when others—including himself—couldn't or wouldn't.

Then he asked them all to look squarely at their father while a special presentation was made to him. The visitor handed the tearful man a lovely ceramic figurine of a soldier, and he said: "This isn't Napoleon; it's just one of his troops. Without the troops, however, there would be few heroes. Never forget the value of one man's willingness to work for the good of others. Never forget your own efforts as part of a team in public service. You may feel financially down at the moment, but your father has given you more than money can buy. He's given you a wonderful example."

That thoughtful neighbor put a father back on a pedestal before his children.

I heard about a group of teenagers in a city neighborhood who organized what they call The Terrific Taxi Team. They sign up for duty and put themselves on call for senior citizens who don't drive anymore but have places they need to go just the same. These youth happily drive the older people to doctor appointments, to the drug store, to a friend's house, to the shopping mall, or along the countryside just for the joy of it. They don't always wait to be called, either. They telephone their clientele and ask if there is any place they can drive them that day. Isn't that great? Here's another example of neighborly goodness.

Carl is the kind of person who is a blessing to a neighborhood. He makes everybody feel good. The countless kindnesses chalked up to his credit are something to shout about, only Carl won't do any shouting. He figures if people need help, somebody ought to help them. And that somebody is often Carl. Some years ago a family whose baby girl suffered from a congenital hip defect moved into his area. She was placed in a body cast and could only lie flat, either on her back or her stomach. She was miserable most of the time and so was everyone else in the family.

One night after Carl had been visiting them, he stayed up very late trying to figure out something that would allow the tiny child to sit upright while the bone-healing took place. Finally, some time later, he was successful. He had rigged a kind of bicycle seat at high-chair level that had special side bars to hold the child securely. The family's life was changed by Carl's caring. Other families in this kind of difficulty wanted an orthochair, too. And Carl obliged. The design was patented later, and now many people have been helped.

Some people ask how they can help, but others just go and do it. In Reno I met a blind girl who was graduating with honors from the university. It hadn't been easy, but she wouldn't have earned her degree at all if there hadn't been good people out there helping. As a freshman she was full of hope that she could do it on her own, but campus life wasn't designed for her kind of problem. One day she stood in the registrar's line waiting to withdraw from school. She passed the time visiting with a stranger she couldn't see.

The problem was shared and a solution was found. The stranger gave hope and counsel to our blind friend. She was not to withdraw from school. She was going to be helped. The new friend would organize some of her Lambda Delta Sigma sorority sisters into shifts of service. They'd take her to class, they'd help her with notes and monitor her projects. That's exactly what they did for four years. When graduation time arrived, the applause for the blind girl was most enthusiastic from all those who had invested their caring into her success. After the ceremony, there was sweet weeping and warm embracing. Oh, what a difference good people can make!

When our children were small, I had serious surgery that proved a trial for a time to our family. Being laid low at the height of the fruit harvest was a frustrating spot for a mother of many to be in. It was worse because we lived in the middle of a small orchard and my bedroom window framed a peach tree burdened with its ripe fruit. Only I couldn't get to it. My husband was out of town on a business emergency, and our helper at home had her hands full with all the little ones. I needed those peaches, and I recall crying silently while I prayed for peace in the face of this waste.

It was while I slept under heavy medication that Bea came to our property and picked the peaches. The next day she returned with nearly sixty quarts of fruit fit, to my marveling eyes, for the state fair exhibit. Only another woman knows the work back of sixty quarts of bottled fruit. Our family ate it with a special kind of reverence all that winter. Well, Bea saw the need and did the deed, and I will love her until I die.

How can we really thank those people who invest their humanity in others? There are no songs of praise sung for them, no news stories today, no name in lights nor a bronze plaque in the hall of fame. Maybe we can only pass our thanks on, as the saying goes, by doing good for someone else ourselves.

Eliza R. Snow, a gifted poetess of the Western pioneer movement, sat with a group of friends for a kind of celebration of compassionate service one to another. This wise woman said, "Let us all watch over each other, that we may sit down in Heaven together."

That is a particularly motivating thought for those of us who are determined to do better in making a difference in life, as so many good people out there are doing.